ONCE IN A GREEN SUMMER

First published in 2001 by Mercier Press
5 French Church Street Cork
Tel: (021) 4275040; Fax: (021) 4274969
E-mail: books@mercier.ie
16 Hume Street Dublin 2
Tel: (01) 661 5299; Fax: (01) 661 8583
E.mail: books@marino.ie

Trade enquiries to CMD Distribution
55A Spruce Avenue
Stillorgan Industrial Park
Blackrock County Dublin
Tel: (01) 294 2560; Fax: (01) 294 2565
E.mail: cmd@columba.ie

© Thomas F. Walsh 2001
ISBN 1 85635 373 7
10 9 8 7 6 5 4 3 2 1

A CIP record for this title is available
from the British Library

Cover design by Mercier Press
Cover photos courtesy of the author
Printed in Ireland by ColourBooks
Baldoyle Industrial Estate, Dublin 13

ONCE IN A GREEN SUMMER

THOMAS F. WALSH

MERCIER PRESS

Contents

Foreign Fields

We got linked up to the Internet for Christmas, and my son, a child of the electronic age, helped me take my first faltering steps onto the information super-highway. I know that if I press the right keys a message will appear from my brother in Wichita, Kansas, four and a half thousand miles away. I had made up my mind that nothing would surprise me, but I was wrong. The surprise was my brother's e-mail address, staring back at me from the screen like a ghost. It read: 'Hygraffa@westwinds.net'. To any Internet user, that term 'Hygraffa' wouldn't mean a thing, but it certainly did to me. My brother had chosen this electronic code word carefully.

High Graffa was the name of a field beside the house where we were born, a field that was all a hill, with a row of hawthorn trees sheltering us from the wild west wind. Our childhood was plotted and pieced in fields, each one with a name and a shape and a history: Gort na Ceartan meant 'the Field of the Forge'. We found old rusted horseshoes there in the red clay as we thinned the turnips.

There was a Low Graffa too, sloping down to the marshy land of Poll na Brafa, where a small stream drained away the floods and a little stone bridge provided a magical place for us to hide our treasure when the dry months of summer came. We hid a quarter-pound of Yorkshire toffees there once, sealed in a biscuit tin, and planned a hoard for the future. But after ten minutes my brother decided that we should only save up hard sweets. We ate the lot and left the tin to rust away forever.

My father knew the measurement of every field, in acres, roods and perches.

'How did they measure them?' I asked him one day as he ploughed the Leath Cheathru. It was such a crooked field that it took all his skill to negotiate the headland.

'Trigonometry,' he answered, with a look of deep wisdom in his eyes and a reverence for those who went before him.

My father loved his fields as if they were a living part of his own body. He remembered their yield and plotted their crop rotation. Under his watchful eye we picked the clover-stones that might damage the mowing machine and pulled up the yellow *bráiste* weed from the green oats in June. He rebuilt the limestone walls when they breached and added to them with the brown rocks that the plough dug up. Here and there he could point out to us the trace of a built-up door, or an ivy-covered archway that once housed a fireplace. *'A time there was, 'ere Ireland's griefs began, When every rood of ground maintained its man,'* he would say.

The only time I ever saw him cry, we were digging potatoes out of the cold wet November soil of Gort a'Lochta beside the road. My brother was leaving home, cycling away, with his suitcase, like his future, balanced precariously in front of him. Maybe my father knew, even then, that this was the end of an era, that, no matter how much he taught us, we would all leave, one by one.

I should be watching the Internet screen now, but I only see Páirc Bheag, the tiny field with the high walls where I used to hide from everything but the sky, and lie on my back among the yellow cowslips and taste the purple clover and look up at the singing lark disappearing in the clouds.

I don't think they have any clouds over Wichita, Kansas – or any fields either, only prairies, stretching away to the end of time. My father wouldn't like that.

I don't blame my own son for getting impatient with me, as we sit staring at the screen, but there is a poem by Monk Gibbon going round and round in my head:

Who would have thought a little field,
A far-off road, a far-off lane,
A far-off cottage could in time
Wake far-off thoughts with so much pain,
Wake far-off thoughts so hard to stem
A man might fear to think of them?

THE SHADOW OF A GUNMAN

Earliest days and nights ease back to me out of uncertainty. Everything seems hushed and muted in soft shadow. I'm about three years of age, tucked into a small box-bed between the big bed where my parents are asleep and the back wall of the house. In the corner, over my head, there's a small four-paned window looking out onto the farmyard. And there's a white moon in the sky, hiding intermittently behind the clouds that race eastwards and the black branches of the hawthorns behind the pigs' stable. Shadows rise and fall on the faded wallpaper. Shapes grow and form and die and my unwritten imagination follows them across the ceiling and into the blacker darkness beyond. There's the low cadence of the wind that drives the clouds and the soft breathing from the big bed beside and above me.

My parents are waiting for sleep to silence me. They are whispering. They probably want some privacy, some time for themselves that does not have to be shared or plundered. Their married life together has been a stumbling journey around interference and interruptions and jealousies and resentment. Their quiet shared moments have had to be short and stolen.

My grandparents had died a few years earlier. At last, my parents would have the whole house to themselves and their children, after twenty-five years of unease and wariness and watching their step, years of being criticised for what they did and how they reared their children and how they did their everyday work. Now, a kind of peace, a new beginning.

'I see a shadow,' I call out in wide-eyed wonder, 'the shadow of a gunman.'

'Go to sleep.'

'Go back to sleep.'

'Be quiet. Be quiet.'

'Go to sleep.'

And sleep comes slowly, and there is quiet, half-suppressed laughter from the big bed in the long, shadow-filled room.

'Where did he hear that?'

'Who told him that?'

'He's hardly able to talk yet.'

'Imagine!'

And they recounted the incident with glee to others, in my hearing, and it marked me as being talkative, someone who would have a way with words maybe. And it seemed to play a part in my forming. It is my very earliest memory.

And fear is an early memory too, and fear shaped me as well. In spite of what our eyes might have told us, we were never alone. We were being watched wherever we went. God was watching us. I toddled around the kitchen with my eyes glued on the eyes of Our Lord in the big picture of the Sacred Heart in the kitchen. It had a small red candle always burning under it, to draw my eyes to the picture. Whether I went towards the fire or the dresser, his eyes were on mine when I looked up. I tried to escape from his relentless gaze, behind the churn or under the table or with a blanket over my head, but every time I dared to look back his eyes were locked on mine, staring back at me. 'You cannot escape,' they said accusingly. 'You are never alone.'

Whenever God's presence waned, empty spaces were peopled by more malignant forces. Ghosts became our childminders, saved us from being lost in the trackless wastes of a wild bog or drowned in a black swallow-hole, or venturing down the slippery stone steps of a well.

'Don't wander off or the fairies will get you.'

'There's a *púca* in that field and he'll get you if you open the gate.'

But there was no way of turning off those forces when it was felt that their guiding hand was not needed. In the enshrouding darkness of the night, when the blackness around was so thick you could almost feel it, when there was no glimmer of a candle or a lamp and when the silence of the night was in itself a sound, those unseen creatures rose out of the edge of my world. A faint glimmer of faded moonlight on a painted door became a spectre and my fearful eyes would be riveted on it, imagining that it was moving and coming towards me. A board in that old house would creak and my heart would stop. And I would cry out and I would be told to go back to sleep, that there was nothing there.

But even in the daytime, the shapes formed by my fearful imagination were durable and tenacious. There was a hen in the yard that struck terror into my soul. She was red and black in colour and she had a sharp, curved yellow beak. I called her the Hag-Hen. Whether she had once caught her comb on a briar or whether it was torn by a cat or dog I do not know, but it hung from her head menacingly, like a witch's hair, and when she strutted towards me I was filled with horror. Panic grabbed me. If I ran, she followed me. My brothers laughed. Everybody laughed. How could you be afraid of a hen? But they did not see her staring eye. They did not look into her evil eye. So I stayed indoors.

I became an observer of what went on in the yard. I would prop myself up inside the small back window of the kitchen and look out, beyond the corner of the scullery, at the cows being driven out of the stables, or my mother coming into the house with pails of milk, or somebody crossing the yard with a *gabhail* of hay. But whenever the Hag-Hen strutted into view, I ducked down until she was gone, so she would not see me.

There were some momentous things that went on in that squared space. I was about three years old when I first witnessed the pig being killed.

There has been a flurry of activity all morning round the house. Cauldrons of water are boiled over the fire, the air of the kitchen fills with damp steam. My father sits inside the front window, sharpening the long pig-knife, scraping it back and forth on the tapered stone, testing the edge every now and then on his thumb. The neighbours coming in, Michael and Joe from next door, their big hobnailed boots noisy on the hearth. A rough hand tossing my hair, asking how I am. 'He's afraid of a hen!' my brother says.

My father is kicking up a fuss, impatient as usual, looking for twine in the jug on the dresser, wanting everything to be ready. Then they all go out and I watch from the window. In the middle of the yard the cart is heeled up, waiting starkly like a gallows. It has been newly painted, bright red and blue, with my father's name and address on the shaft: 'M. Walsh, Carrowbeg'.

The pig is pulled by the hind leg from the pigs' stable on the far side of the yard. He is roaring for all his might, as if he knows his impending fate. Joe, a cigarette dangling from his lips, has the pig's hind leg in a firm grip. Joe is a joker, he laughs at everything. This is a laugh for him. They lift the pig onto the cart, its head down towards the lower end. The men hold it, belly up, while its hind legs are lashed with lengths of rope to the hind shafts. There is a man holding each front leg as my father ties the pig's jaws shut with twine so that its roaring becomes a sharp, ear-splitting, incessant whine. My mother has her scarf on her head and is going out with the white pail. I can tell she is nervous. She crouches, holding the pail under the pig's head. I see the shining steel of the blade plunge into the white, upturned neck and the red blood burst out and spray and spatter and turn into a steady stream

14

into the pail. My mother's head is turned away. The shuddering of the white body slows down and the sharp whine dies in the air. Joe, the neighbour, finishes his cigarette. It is a long time before the blood stops flowing.

Later, my mother led me by the hand as she carried another pail of steaming water out to the barn. I clutched the tails of my mother's long coat for comfort, looking fearfully around for any signs of the Hag-Hen. The double doors of the barn were wide open. The pig was hanging from a cross-beam, its head over the big round galvanised tub. Its grinning teeth were bared in a fixed agony, blood dripping through its mouth and nostrils. The floor of the barn was covered in fresh straw and the scrubbed kitchen table was in the middle of the floor.

My father and the other men were scraping the hair from the skin with knives, sluicing the pink and white body with hot water. They were all talk and merriment but my eyes were fixed on the pig's eyes. They were glazed and unmoving. They did not look back at me, but through me, as if I was not there. They locked onto my gaze, and I could not look away until my mother dragged me off through the open doors and back into the house for another pail of water.

When we came back out, the pig's belly had been split right open, down the middle, from its curly little tail to the throat where my father had first plunged the sharp blade. The inside of the pig was as empty as a cave, and the sides were kept open by three or four hazel scallops. I peeped over the edge into the tub and it was half-full of red snake-like things and gooey bulbous stuff and even some of the pig's dirt, and it made me shudder to look at it.

My mother plunges her arm into all that awful mess and fishes out the puddings and puts them in the pail and I'm watching her face while she's doing it and I can see that she's disgusted but she still does it. My brother Michael is playing with a white round thing full of air and I know it came from the pig. 'Look, it's the bladder,' he says, and sticks it in my face and I scream at the cold wet smell of it and I run to the house alone and I don't even think of the Hag-Hen. I just want to be safe by the fire.

ANNIE LEE

My mother's name was Annie Lee, and she was born and reared in Carnacrow House. She was a tall, slender woman, with refined features and a mild manner that belied a resolute mind. Her father made his money in America, and bought the big house and a couple of hundred acres from an impecunious landlord. He married my grandmother, who had worked as a nurse in Australia. They were better off than most of the people, and Granny Lee wanted her children to be well off too. She had three sons and five daughters. The eldest boy, Walter, looked after the farm. She sent her two younger boys to boarding school. One of them, my Uncle Thomas, went on to study medicine in University College Galway before he ran away and joined the Irish Guards in London. Uncle Michael, the youngest boy, had that kind of sensitive intelligence that tends towards anxiety and nervousness. He became desperately unhappy in boarding school and came home to work on the farm, resigning himself to a life of quiet toil where he had to shoulder no responsibility. He was a tall, gangling, stooped man with a bony face, who knew the works of Shakespeare and Milton's *Paradise Lost,* and whose memory was so good that his word on day and date was final. He contented himself with local lore and laughed as he quoted the simple anecdotes that made others laugh around him, but sometimes you could notice, if he looked over a wall or shielded his eyes against the sun, that he had a lost look in his eye, and though he never talked about himself, I often got the feeling that there was a ghost that hovered over him.

Granny Lee had done well in Australia. She had saved enough money to be a suitable match for her husband. She visited auctions at the great houses, from which landlords were pulling out in that time of agrarian agitation. She bought fine furniture for Carnacrow. She moved up a step on the ladder. Now she was anxious that her daughters should do well also. The eldest became a nurse, like her mother, and emigrated to Australia. There was a match made for the second girl, Bridget – a placid, good-looking girl – when she was twenty-two years old. She was to marry a man twenty years her senior, whom she had never seen before. He had a good holding of land, about eighty acres, in Cahermacnally. They had eight children before he died in his sleep. Then she took to the bed for good, never rising except for weddings, funerals or other auspicious occasions. When I visited her as a child she spoke in a high-pitched voice from the bed, her skin white as snow, her head always covered with some kind of hat. My brother said it was a tea cosy.

My mother, at the age of nineteen, did not want to meet the same fate as her older sister, married to someone she did not know or love, her whole life mapped out before her without her choosing. She loved reading and she loved poetry, and she read books that her mother had bought in job lots at auctions. Curled up in bed at night, in the high-ceilinged bedroom in Carnacrow, reading by candlelight, she opened hard-backed books of poetry and fiction that had been the proud possession of some landlord who had to sell out and leave for India or South Africa, books like William Blake's *Songs of Innocence and Experience,* with its fantastical drawings, and her imagination danced and soared with the flickering flame of the candle and the weaving shadows around her. She became a lover of romance and heroism and bravery and all the things that books are full of.

When she was sixteen years old, Ireland became a land where heroes and bravery had their time and space. It was 1921, and the Black and Tans and Auxiliaries were roaming the countryside. My father's cousin, also called Michael Walsh, owned a public house in Galway called The Old Malt. He was the Sinn Féin chairman of Galway Urban District Council. Five men with English accents called to his door one night, marched him back to The Long Walk, shot him through the right ear and threw him into the docks. My father went to the funeral, and his name appeared in the paper as one of the mourners. There was an ambush of an Auxiliary patrol at Alcorn's mill, outside the town of Headford, and several of the Cadets were wounded. The next day they returned in a convoy of lorries and set fire to the town. They drove through the sur-rounding countryside and shot three young men who were working in the fields. They drove past Carnacrow House and shot another man called William Walsh, who was no relation of ours. My father did not sleep at home those nights, but in a dugout under a wooden bridge in the bog in Knocklahard.

At this time a knock came on the door in Carnacrow and a young man with sandy hair, dressed in an officer's uniform of the Irish Volunteers, presented himself to my grandfather. He was the Commandant of the Flying Column, North Galway Brigade, of the IRA and he was looking for lodgings for his officers and men. There were about twenty-five of them in all. Granny and Grandad argued and debated as to what to do. My mother listened from her bedroom door.

'What if the Tans come and they're here?'

'If we refuse, maybe they'll burn the house over our heads!'

'If the British come, they'll burn it also, and maybe the rest of us in it!'

But my grandfather, apparently, had his way in the end: 'If it was your son that was out there, wouldn't you want someone to take him in?'

They stayed for a week, the men sleeping in the loft over the barn, the four officers in the spare bedroom. They were polite and gentle in their speech and refined in their manner, and my mother fell for Frank, the commandant. They gathered round the piano in the parlour at night and they sang. They sang songs of freedom like 'God Save Ireland' and 'Wrap the Green Flag Round Me, Boys', but the sandy-haired leader sang 'The Shawl of Galway Grey' in a fine tenor voice and with such feeling that everybody was affected by its pathos:

'Twas soft the night we parted,
Too quickly came the day,
When silent, broken-hearted,
I went from you away.

The dawn was breaking o'er Glen Rua,
It stole the stars away,
The last fond look I caught of you
In your shawl of Galway grey.

My mother felt that he sang the song especially for her, that his eyes were on her, and she took the words into her heart and nurtured them there. I think she might have fallen in love with him, not just with him, but also with the idea of him.

She woke up one morning to find that the flying column had left. Granny and Grandad made a small fire in the haggard and burned any traces that remained, though there were very few: some empty cigarette packets and a few discarded articles of clothing.

Annie must have been deeply affected by this exciting episode in her otherwise uneventful existence. For a week she had stepped into another world, a world of idealism and brashness and swaggering bravery. She had met and sung with heroes, and her own world would never be the same.

She read and reread 'The Lady of Shallot' and she learned it and it went round in her head all day. She fastened on a long poem in the collected works of John Greenleaf Whittier called 'The Ballad of Maud Muller'. It is about a young rustic girl who falls in love with a rich and powerful judge. The judge rides by the hayfield where she works on a summer's day and stops to ask her for a drink of water from the well. He falls in love with her beauty and simplicity, and the vision of her and her uncomplicated life haunts him. Yet they follow their own inevitable paths that destiny has laid down for them:

> *He wedded a wife of richest dower,*
> *Who lived for fashion, as he for power*

while

> *She wedded a man unlearned and poor,*
> *And many children played round her door.*

And the judge and the country maiden both lived the rest of their lives with the gnawing pain of regret. My mother learned that poem so well that it became part of her. She could say the verses and tell the story to me many years later, and their telling welled out of a great sadness. Her sweet, soft recitation haunts me still:

> *Then she took up her burden of life again,*
> *Saying only, "It might have been."*
> *Alas for maiden, alas for Judge,*
> *For rich repiner and household drudge!*
>
> *God pity them both! and pity us all,*
> *Who vainly the dreams of youth recall.*
> *For of all sad words of tongue or pen,*
> *The saddest are these: "It might have been!"*

22

When the Black and Tans left, and the black shadow of Civil War spread quickly across the small towns and the fields and the families that worked them, the flying column that had criss-crossed the lanes and byways of north Galway split up and was re-formed into a band of Irregulars, vehemently opposed to any treaty with the British. Frank became one of these Irregulars, as did the other three officers who had drunk tea and sung their ballads round the piano in the parlour in Carnacrow. In February 1923, they were surrounded and captured by Free State troops in Clúid and thrown into Galway Jail. In April in that same year, in one of the last engagements of that bloody feud – one of the last actions in the whole of Ireland – the Military Barracks in Headford (the building that is now the Bank of Ireland) was attacked by the Irregulars. It was a bloody battle, and after it men lay dying in the street. Two days later, in direct reprisal for that action, six of the men who had been captured in Clúid, Frank among them, were shot at dawn in Tuam by government forces. The people knew it was going to happen. My mother rose at dawn and went alone to the high Chapel Field, where she could see the grey dawn spread its cold light over the bare fields. She remembered the sandy-haired commandant and she remembered the words of the song:

The dawn was breaking o'er Glen Rua,
It stole the stars away,

The last fond look I caught of you,
In your shawl of Galway grey.

She often went out alone on those early-morning walks to the Chapel Field, seeing in those flickering glimpses of broken sunrise a fleeting fragment of a life that had visited her once and once only. A dream, maybe, but a kind of a wound as well, a vision that had entered like a surgeon's knife and left a scar that would heal but that would always be there.

About a year later, on one of those walks, she wandered out, dressed in a white calico dress, to the Chapel Field again to watch the sun rise. She was startled to see a man, dressed in a long black coat, leaning against a wall, with a gun by his side. My father was a handsome man, about six foot in height, with strong features and a mischievous smile. But whenever she spoke about their first meeting, it was clear that it was his dancing blue eyes that attracted her most of all, the way they looked into her, not shyly like other local men, but steadily and boldly, as if daring her to turn her back and walk away.

They met there in the ring of beech trees, many stolen mornings; she, padding softly across the landing by her sleeping parents, across the flagged floor of the big kitchen in Carnacrow House, out to the shady bower where he would be waiting by the wall. There she would embrace him, her thin body in the cool white calico dress and he, strong and muscular in his rough frieze jacket, his bright blue eyes shining under the shadow of his cloth cap.

Later that same year, Granny Lee made plans for Annie. She was to be matched with a wealthy farmer like her sister Bridget. She made up her mind quickly.

Without the knowledge of either set of parents, she and Mick went to the parish priest and told him that they were 'keeping company' and that they wanted to get married. They were married secretly in Claran Church in August 1925. She was exactly twenty years old. He was twenty-five. They went to lodgings in Galway and waited for tempers to die down at home. Granny and Granda Lee were furious and refused to give her a dowry of any kind. She was not welcome in Ivy Cottage without bringing any money into the place, but after some time they took the young couple in. The only possession she had apart from the clothes on her back was an old leather writing case full of letters and photographs.

There was resentment and bitterness between the two families for a while. After several months had elapsed, Annie went to Carnacrow and demanded what she felt was rightfully hers. Her parents finally relented and gave her a hundred and fifty pounds and a walnut chiffonier. That was her furniture.

The money that she brought into Carrowbeg was given directly to my father's sister, as her dowry, so that she could leave Ivy Cottage and make her own way in the world. Annie settled in to a life of hard work and dedication to her husband and family. She reared ten children. She cooked and sewed and milked the cows and cleaned out the byre. She helped in the fields when the need arose. Eight of her ten children were born before my father's parents passed on. She worked her fingers to the bone and her selfless love knew no bounds. She grew to be very content, but there were old songs that made her sad, and when we visited her old home there was a wistfulness in the way she talked. Our journeys back home were always marked by a quiet sadness.

Going with my mother to visit the house where she was born was a real adventure for me as a child. It was the biggest house I had ever seen, a two-storey thatched giant with two enormous Tudor chimneys. We went up a tree-lined avenue for a half-mile and in through the Grand Gate to the huge lawn in front of the house. The lawn was interspersed with great swaying ash trees that groaned and creaked in the wind. The cropped grass was dotted with bunches of daffodils in the springtime.

There were nine high windows to the front of the whitewashed house, each with twelve small panes of glass. The hall door had a great big brass knocker.

The first thing you saw when my aunt Sarah, Walter's wife, opened the hall door was a stuffed badger on a bamboo stand. My aunt hung my box-pleated coat on an ivory hatstand, but I kept my eyes on the badger for fear it would go for me. The hall had a wooden floor, and my aunt's heavy shoes made a thundering sound as she walked across it.

She would lead us into the stone-floored kitchen and my Uncle Michael would be sitting beside the huge open fireplace smoking his pipe. He was old the first time I ever saw him. It seemed to me as if God had given him teeth that were a size too big. He had great difficulty closing his lips on his pipe. Though he was very clever, talk came very slowly to him as he puffed on the pipe. The spaces between words were filled with the tick-tock from the old pendulum clock on the wall. Through the lace curtains you could see the swallows darting to their nests in the barn. The rooks clamoured from the high branches of the ash trees on the lawn.

Sometimes, if it was Christmas time or a special occasion, Aunt Sarah would bring us into the parlour. I would get a glass of diluted orange and my mother would have a glass of sherry.

The parlour was a wondrous place. By the window, there was the piano that Aunt Winifred used to play. In the alcove by the white marble fireplace there was a cabinet with glass shelves full of green Beleek figurines and dainty little china cups. The walls were covered in heavily embossed wallpaper and hung with old sepia-coloured photographs. There was a lace tablecloth on the polished oval dining table in the middle of the room.

This was a room that held time captive. The High Sheriff of Galway built it, before he fell on hard times and had to sell. My grandmother furnished it, with money saved in Australia. This is where my mother and her sisters entertained the officers of the flying column, while the private soldiers slept outside in the barn. This is where they sang 'Oft in the Stilly Night' and 'God Save Ireland'. But those old songs only made my mother sad now, and I'm sure she trembled inwardly at the sight of that polished parlour.

Carnacrow House fell to wrack and ruin when the old people died. Somebody stripped the thatch off the roof and slated it with red tiles. But I still have my mother's writing case, and the blotting paper holds the imprint of her maiden name.

EARLY SHAPES

My early view of the world was full of female forms. I had four older sisters around the house. They petted and cuddled and washed and scrubbed and scolded and saved me from the perils of the house. They filled my head with warnings of things that would get me if I wandered to the top of the stairs alone, then, when it suited them, they assured me that the shapes I saw in the wall upstairs were only the dark spaces between stones, that the sounds I heard in the black night were the dry rafters stretching themselves and cracking like Auntie Mollie's bones.

On Saturday night the big wooden tub, wheeled in from the scullery, was filled with scalding water, and the flannel cloth, bubbling with Sunlight soap, was twisted into every orifice, high up and low down, all over my protesting body. My sisters did the scrubbing, and they did it with a vengeance. They hated it as another thankless chore, and they took their temper out on us small boys, Michael, Jim and I. They rubbed us raw, they ignored our squeals about soap in our eyes and carried on until we emerged, shivering in front of the blazing fire, our skin like a fresh pork steak.

My mother was wary of all the illnesses that might prey on us. She brought me out to the haggard one day and watched and waited while I crouched behind the stack of corn. Finally I obliged, and my bowels moved. She poked through it with a stick and said 'Aha! I thought so.' I took a peep and nearly fainted with horror. White worms wriggling and twisting. I thought I was going to die. The remedies for such ailments were always dire to the taste and a worse prospect than death itself. There was Glauber's Salts, which loosened us up after any overindulgence in hazelnuts had bound our guts like a vice. There was Aungier's Emulsion and Radio Emulsion and gripe water, all of them so disgusting that they would make your gorge rise. Whenever we got boils on our necks they were promptly treated with a bread poultice so hot that you screamed in agony, but just to make sure you suffered properly, the boil was then squeezed between the thumbs until the pus spurted out.

When I was very little I contracted scarlet fever. The doctor came and ordered that I be separated from the other children in the house. A special bed was made up for me in my parents' room. I was swaddled in a ton of blankets and rugs. My nights were feverish. The walls and ceiling turned to rubber and warped and swayed around me. I saw ghoulish shapes coming to take me away. The sheets burned under me like a sea of lighted paraffin. I tossed in sleepless turmoil all night, my mother mopping my forehead with a cool cloth. I slept in the early mornings and awoke in the pallid afternoons limp and languid as a slug, in puzzlement as to who or where I was. Slowly, over weeks, my strength returned, my legs held me up at last, and I could sit by the fire and drink soup from a mug.

My Aunt Mollie, my father's sister, I remember as a barely moving black shape by the fire, with pure white hair in crinkly curls and a benign smile that welcomed us wordlessly when we brought her handfuls of cowslips or buttercups from the hazy fields. She was a simple soul, always mellow and quiet in her talk, welcoming us into her ample lap like a brood of yapping puppies. She seldom left the hearth, and like a friendly household god she blessed our childish labours. God created her simple and uncluttered with human guile. She laughed in the face of anger and despair. She gazed through the open door in the summertime at the far-off shimmering hills of Kilroe as if she was looking at something none of the rest of us could ever see. Her horizons were far beyond ours, and there was a kind of a smile she had that told us, as we gazed up from her lap, that she really lived in another world.

I was too small to remember the details of her dying. She just left the stage of my childhood house. There was a space at the side of the hearth and an unexpected emptiness in the crowded house.

My early toddling days took me stumbling out of doors on summer mornings when the sunlight hung in a golden gauze of mist about the front door. I would follow a yellow butterfly until it bounced on its airy springs over the little garden wall. The flower garden in front of the ivied house was tiny, walled off from the marauding hens, with a pebbled path set out in cruciform. If I turned left outside the front door, there was an iron gate that I could not open. Straight in front of the house, the path led smack into a low, flat-topped wall, which to me at the time seemed as high as a mountain. If I took a turn right, the narrow path led up three steps to a curved, raised area under a huge copper beech tree that swayed and whispered to the clouds in the blue sky above it. Those toddling days were days of looking up and longing, longing to be able to climb into the smooth, shaded branches of that tree, or to run along that flat-topped garden wall like my brothers, shouting at the sky and flailing arms into the wind instead of being sheltered from it.

There were roses in the garden, peony roses in two heart-shaped beds, and there were tall asters by the wall and yellow rambling roses too that lost their stems in the thick green ivy of the house and appeared again, high up, to frame the dark doorway in summer with a crown of colour.

By the stone steps of the raised lawn there was a purple lilac tree, or rather a bush, for it had many shoots that sprang from the corner of the house. The wall that divided this part of the raised garden from the haggard behind it was taller, and there was a cavernous, shaded spot, on top of the wall, that my eldest sister called her bower, where she hid and read, and held her finger to her lips as she saw me looking up, quizzically, from the path below.

Mary never liked the drudgery of work about the fields or the farmyard. What she liked to do was devour books. She read while she rocked my cradle, she read while she milked the cows in the stable, she read in bed with a flashlamp and at the first upward gush of lemon-coloured dawn through the small window of her room. She was tall and willowy, with skin as white as bog-cotton and tight black curls, intelligent and quick-witted and never lost for an answer. She cycled the three miles to secondary school in Headford when she could manage to get a bicycle that worked. At the best of times the wheels had solid rubber tyres that shook the guts out of her on the rutted road. At the worst of times she walked in rain and wind and sun.

She usually got the job, in those rationed war years, of scouring the village for commodities that were not available. There would be no tea, or no paraffin for the lamp, or no candles to be got anywhere. When she came home empty-handed to a houseful of children, she got blamed.

She got a job in the civil service when she was sixteen and went off to live in Dublin. We young ones missed her around the house. Her sharp wit was revered: her haughty air, big words and good-humoured sarcasm. I missed her shape from the shady bower under the lilac bush; her pale face looking down at me, her finger to her lips.

Cecile was two years younger than Mary. She was strong and big-boned and serious, and because my oldest brother Charlie was away in college, she had to do the man's work around the farm. She learned to plough with the horses, and spring-harrow, and she carried bags of wheat on her back into the barn and could throw a sheaf of oats as far as any man. She never complained about scuffling or sowing turnips or taking the donkey to mix hand-turf in the muck-filled swamp of the bog in Knocklahard. She rooped potatoes out of the frosty soil when piercing autumn fog wrung the heat out of her blood. She pulled nettles and docks out of the stony clay of the beet field in the draining heat of summer. Her nails were cracked and broken like any man's, her skin weathered like a piece of shiny leather, but she did not seem to mind. My father loved her, praised her and sang of her strength and endurance.

During the days of compulsory tillage, every second field in that patchwork valley seemed to be turned brown. Even headlands seemed precious; people steered the plough close to the wall to eke out another inch. My father took conacre from my mother's Uncle Thomas in Culleen, in a farm once opulent but now neglected. The fields were wide, rolling pastures and the farm buildings were of cut stone. My father, Cecile and my brother Pat, who was now in his early teens, hauled ploughs and harrows there, lifting them on and off the horse cart to tear open pastures that were rough and stony and relentless. They were a team: my father a brute-force tamer and breaker, my sister a quiet, sturdy second-in-command, soothing his rage. The coulter cleaved coarse wiry grassland into fine blackness. Together they planted and weeded and cut corn and hauled it home in high-piled swaying carts by the house, and the yard was filled with the crunch of cartwheels and the grunting of horses. The haggard was piled with stands and stacks of corn and there were potatoes rumbling from heeled-up carts with a sound like thunder rolling in the hills. They were poured into pits and wrapped in sheltering straw and coats of clay and dried stalks to withstand the biting winter frosts. There seemed to be mounds of yellow mangolds and round purple turnips in every corner.

I emerged into this world falling and stumbling over the plentiful bounty of the earth, climbing hazardous heaps of mangolds that gave way under me or landed on my head as I dislodged them. I bit into the pink flesh of turnips and tasted their sweetness. I lost myself in caves of piled straw and sat silent in the sheltered hidden yellowness watching the light filter through the webbed world and listening to the clicking language of silence that surrounded me. Then, all of a sudden, I would panic at the thought of the sharp prongs of a fork being plunged thoughtlessly into me, or that maybe a sudden cartload of straw would be piled on me and I would be buried in a silent tomb, alone and lost to those who searched and called out, oblivious to my muffled cries.

More Sisters

Una was the third-eldest sister, and she was a sultry beauty, with cascading brown hair and bright blue eyes that lit up the deepest of shadows around her. Her eyes had the timid sadness of a puppy, a look that pleaded for gentleness and understanding. Ephemeral as thistledown, she was the apple at the top of the tree, sweet and inaccessible. You could never imagine her lifting rocks in the field or dosing lambs or cleaning out the pigs' stable. She was much too fine for that. I don't know how she eased herself away from asperity, how she glided by everything that was savage around her. Maybe she hid behind the cushions in the parlour when the pig was being killed or the stables cleaned, until eventually my father was conditioned into leaving her alone. Perhaps he saw in her the same gentility that my mother once undoubtedly had, until hardship and grinding necessity and the spectre of poverty calloused her hands and coated her soft kernel with the hard shell of drudgery. Perhaps he saw in his daughter's soft eyes the perpetuation of that gentility of spirit that had once attracted and refined him.

So I remember Una, a gilded, teenage girl gliding round the house, her brown, shoulder-length hair tumbling over her slender shoulders, going to the well in Poll na Brafa for water and carrying in the turf for the fire. I see her sitting, hunched, on the stone steps that led down to the water and gazing into its depth as if it was the dreamy future. She would linger, her dirndl dress floating in the windy waves of a meadow, picking languorously at the stamens of a purple clover while the slow-munching cows made a curious circled audience around her. When she had finished with the flower, something would flicker on the blue mirror of her dreaming eye and she would smile a wistful smile, dreaming, perhaps, of being a lady.

She got by in primary school as unobtrusively as she did on the farm, without bothering too much about hard sums or anything as tedious as the *Modh Coinn-íollach*. One flicker of her dark lashes told Master Garvey to leave her alone. She danced nimbly around her lessons, picking up what she wanted, like a housewife at a market stall. When the time came, she was decked out in a white starched blouse and a black pencil skirt and sent in to McCormack's Hotel, and she began to find her place in a great world that did not include spreading cow manure or scuffling turnips. She blossomed like a white rose in the sun. She came home with gushing tales of high society, of Molly O'Rourke sipping gin and tonic and the Galway Blazers having hot port before the hunt and Joe Fair actually talking to her as he sat smiling at the polished mahogany bar. There were dinner dances and socials and subterfuges and covert happenings all around her, but she remained an innocent abroad, as impervious to staining as the cut glass in that crumbling relic of old graciousness.

By this time, space at home was at a premium. Beds were fully booked; we slept, for the most part, head to toe. When I was about two years old, I graduated from the cot beside my parents to the humid warmth of my sisters' bed, and slept curled up in cosy roundness with a relay of my sisters like a pet lamb in the flock. I was happy there, with the smell of lavender and perfumed talcum powder hanging in the air around me. I was cuddled and cosseted and cared for and lulled to sleep each night with a hushed female reassurance that nothing would appear from the woven rafters overhead or leap out at me from a crack in the wall.

Then came the day when I was banished to the cold austerity of the boys' bedroom, where everything was rough and tumble like a calves' stable and where I had to fend for myself or be trampled to death. I slept with the older twin boys, at the foot of their bed, with the smell of their toes in my face and their frequent, deliberate farts to taunt and tease me. They took delight in making me afraid in the soupy darkness, convincing me when the dog howled that it was the banshee wailing as she washed her clothes at the stream in Poll na Brafa, or pointing out the Púca Tree on the dim horizon on the twist of the road to Baby Ellen's and stoking my wide-eyed fear with tales of a man hanged there for murder. It would lead to a nightmare-ridden sleep, in which I was carried off by a headless horseman to a dark cave. I was about to be mutilated when I would wake up, shivering, in a pool of cold sweat, to the snores of my brothers above me and their bony ankles round my ears.

My brother Pat was two years younger than Una; then came the next girl, Rose, a tousle-haired bundle of good humour and a torment and eternal tease to us younger boys. When she was bored, which was often, she thought up new and vicious ways to make us mad. She herself was frustrated by being lumbered with the weight of looking after us, the three youngest boys, washing our feet on a Saturday night in the tub in front of the fire, scrubbing behind our ears and drying our hair, polishing our shoes and leaving them in a row inside the front door. She helped my mother wash the clothes and starch the collars and hang out the washing and cook for her father and brothers. She had to help in the fields, turning hay and picking potatoes and thinning beet. She was at everybody's beck and call and it frustrated her and made her feel like a skivvy and a drudge, but her sunny humour saved her soul from bitterness.

Everything we did, every skill and chore, every sheaf we tied and every seedling we thinned and every back-breaking sod of turf we turned to the sun was done to the background of her taunting, mocking, tumbling laughter. The cleverness of her own sarcasm made her crease with laughter and made us cringe like kittens.

The Hearth and Stool and All

The huge fireplace was lord of the kitchen. It was the sun of our solar system, we revolved around it, revered it, yearned for its warmth and comfort. The spark of life in it was our spark of life, and it was never allowed to die. It was raked at night, the last embers of drowsy slumber-time covered carefully with ashes from the pit under the hob and then, when cold dawn beckoned, the glowing red coals were disinterred and kindled into flame with dry turf and twigs. Then the kitchen and the whole house breathed life again and warmth spread outwards over the cold floor.

In those rare moments when the fire was low, I could lean in over it and look up past the turn in the dark chimney and just make out the square of sky above, and sometimes even see a cloud passing, as if through the shutter of a camera. There was always the salty smell of soot and the equally sweet smell of the turf and the sigh of the wind in the hollowness above. Here was my domain as a child, around this hearth, never straying far from it, knowing instinctively that under its wide protective arch was everything I needed, food and heat and shelter and human love. Here, wedged in the hob over the warm ashes, I watched the first rituals of life move around me.

My mother was queen and ruler of the fireplace, swinging the iron crane out, hanging a big black kettle on it until it spouted steam hissing into the red coals underneath, or hauling a huge cauldron of potatoes to the fire to be boiled for the pigs. She would carry it half-supported on her knee, the weight of it bending her. She would rest her elbows on her knees as she crouched in front of the fire, with the long tongs in her expert hand, standing the turf in circles, breaking the grey coals into life, piling them on the lid of the bread oven, coaxing flames from nowhere.

It was a big kitchen to me then, with a long, padding, barefoot walk to the dresser at the other end. The dresser was the other ruler of that wide living space, the fire's antithesis, the focus of attention when the light shone and you could turn from the heat. It was a wooden leviathan, taking over the whole wall space between the stairs and the bedroom door, high as the ceiling, shelves shining with plates and jugs and cups and saucers, doors and drawers hiding enough artefacts to fill a haberdashery. It was made on the spot by a genius of a carpenter, my father said, a man who could saw three planks at once and never had to measure anything.

There were three high shelves on the upper part of the dresser, and on the highest of them, in front of the big willow-pattern dishes, stood a row of eight jugs, all different in design and shape, arranged according to size, from the big jug with the pink stripe on the right to the little Forget-Me-Not on the left. They were never placed on the table, never taken from behind the light rail that kept them safe. They stood for family pride and prestige and as a testimony to a kind of indestructible civility. They were acquired and paid for and passed on and admired in the way that jewels or silver might be in another realm. Different people had bought them and they were named in their honour and memory. There was a Grandma's jug and a jug that came from America. There was history in the jugs' ordered rank.

Above all else, however, the jugs on our dresser were the family filing cabinet, the loading pen and burial ground of all lost and wayward things. There was a plan, of course. In the big jug with the pink stripe you should find the receivable orders, demand notes and rate receipts. This was the tabernacle of jugs, the holy of holies. If my father went there and did not find what he wanted, all hell would break loose. The second jug, the next in size and hierarchy, was for the ration book and the dog licence and other less ponderous documents. If you put your hand into the pansy jug with the scalloped edge, you would find some plant seed, the pellets for the calves, and a stick of sealing wax for the knots on a parcel. There was never a guarantee that things would be where they were supposed to be, but as you went down the line of jugs things became even more vague and haphazard. There were things vital to the smooth running of everyday life that were hard to categorise. If you groped into a jug hoping to find a connection for the bicycle pump, you might get a sharp prod of a packing needle instead, or if you were sent in from the yard in a hurry to get the pig rings, you might have to empty all the jugs out one by one on the kitchen table before finding them.

Below the jugs there was a shelf of cups and saucers interspersed with eggcups, and below that again the broad lap of the dresser, dressed in a glossy bright oilcloth, with serrated trim hanging over the edge. Here was a jumble of delights: a cottage teapot, a china hen that was really a butter dish, a round tin with a hole at the top which usually held a ball of twine. Here would go on display for a short time the cartwheels of brown-and-white soda bread that my mother baked on the bounteous hearth. They would hardly have time to cool before being loaded on to the table and devoured with warm milk and sugary tea and butter that was beaten gold.

Those jugs and plates and crockery that the big old dresser held, shone in the lamplight like the treasures of a china stall. Their glaze was cracked and fissured like the parched surface of the desert and some of the cutlery in the big drawer was bronzed and bent, but they held a quiet aura of incorruptible age about them, as if they were the veterans of an old and honourable war.

The oil lamp hung high on the left side of the arch over the fire, its beams dying by the dresser between the front door and the big cross door which led to the scullery. Between those two doors, on the border between light and shadow, was the arena where my brothers and I played, darting between the goalpost doors, hearing the roar of the crowd from the grandstand that was the dresser, dodging swinging pots being carried to the fire and pails of milk left to cool for skimming, tripping over wellingtons and broom. We vanished into the shadows if my father growled and glared from his big Windsor chair under the lamp. If he reached for his cap, alarm bells rang. He would hold the cloth cap half folded, the speck curved into a club, and could bring it down with amazing accuracy and force onto the top of our skulls – that little unprotected spot where the hair began to grow. He called it 'a crop on the *cúl',* and it was a major deterrent against childish pranks.

These pranks were often ingenious. My father liked to light his pipe when he settled into his big chair after the toil of the fields. He would pick up a red twig from the fire or a scrap of paper that might be lying about. We would unscrew the lamp wick, dip a few folded pieces of newspaper into the paraffin and leave them lying innocently on the floor near his chair. We would dip them in such a way that the two ends of the paper were dry and the middle was soaked in oil. When he stooped to light the paper in the fire, it burned naturally for a few seconds, then, halfway to the pipe, it would explode into a ball of light. 'God blast it!' he would shout, throwing it from him and tipping his tobacco onto his waistcoat. We could not laugh out loud, but we would melt into the shadows and build into a pressure cooker of unexploded mirth, holding our noses to keep it in.

Everybody, in those days of innocence, played tricks; some of these people were children, and some were not so young. Once, after threshing, when the men were at the table, my sisters were pouring tea and cutting wedges of soda bread, and my mother was carrying boiled eggs to the table in her apron, Michael Charlie said aloud above the stirring of tea, 'Look at the lovely pocket watch I found in the haggard', and he pulled from his waistcoat pocket a live field mouse tied by a shoelace to the button of his coat, and let it scamper among the cups. My sister poured the hot tea onto my father's lap. My mother jumped two feet off the ground, and the boiled eggs went everywhere across the room. My father could not lose his temper with a neighbour who had sweated for him all morning. He suffered the scald, forced a smile, shook his head and resigned himself to the old gods of humour.

'The devil o' the likes of ye!' he said.

It was in this arena that I grew strong enough to face the outside world.

The Butt of the Wind

'Literature begins with the telling
of a tale.'

ARTHUR KOESTLER

At the misty, blurred edge of my earliest memories,
when there was silence all around, and shadow, and
softness in that shadow, I remember stories, stories
read and stories told from the heart, where they had
been stored from generations gone by. Stories that
spurred my imagination and carried me on a wild ride
across the dark sky to places that became more
powerful and vivid and real for me than the world of
shadow I inhabited.

I sat on Mollie's lap, her arm around me, the other
hand on the tongs stirring the fire into flame, her white
hair like strings of wool against the darkness of the
smoky ceiling. She had a story that she had learned
from her mother. It was called 'The Butt of the Wind',
and she told it like a poem that had repeating lines
that echoed and resonated and nailed it to the memory.
She pronounced 'wind' in the old country way, as if it

rhymed with 'find', and every thing or person that was small had the Irish suffix *'-ín'*. The story was all about a little boy who set out to cut the butt of the wind because his mother was perished with the cold, and in the picture-forming blankness of my mind the wind was then – and in a way forever – shaped like a tree, with a butt or stem that you could cut and a burgeoning top whose branches were storms and gales and winter blizzards. The boy on his journey met the King of Connaught, who persuaded him not to cut the wind and gave him a magic *'potín'* to which he had to say, *'Potín, potín,* bake up *cakíns*', and the magic pot would bake up all the wondrous cakes imaginable, and there was a villain in the story and everything seemed to happen three times and every time that Mollie told me the story, looking with her dreamy eyes into the fire, the words would be exactly the same. It was a story as old and as shaped as the fields, at home with the smell of turf-smoke and the red flames of the fire and the grey-haired woman stooping by the fire, passing on something from her childhood to a child of a new age. It was as magical a potion as the magic it told. I had no picture of the magisterial King of Connaught except the one my imagination drew on the whiteness of my mind's eye; no special effects except those seen in the flames of the fire into which I stared.

We were read to as children, after washing in the galvanized tub and supper of soda bread and milk. We sat with shins to the fire and watched the scrubbed skin turn a mottled red. The first book I remember was *The Children of the New Forest* by Captain Marryatt.

I still remember the names of the four children whose father was killed by the Roundheads: Edward, Humphrey, Alice and Edith, and how they were saved from their burning house and brought to live in the forest by an old forester called Jacob Armitage. He taught the boys how to hunt deer and the girls how to sow vegetables and cook and clean, and he taught them, too, how to pull together and survive on frugality, and it all seemed to us then so appropriate and so right. We longed to be like those boys hunting deer in the forest and hiding from the Roundheads and following imperceptible trails. I can see, through the mist of hundreds of forgotten books that I have since read, some of the illustrations from that old, well-thumbed book. Edward, a boy dressed in strange Cavalier clothes, holding his hands to heaven and crying, 'Has all England gone craven?' And I can see another illustration of an arm poking through a small window to shoot a pistol. In the sleepy hollow of our feather beds we dreamed the lives of those Cavalier children from another age and another history, and the following day we lived their lives, shouting to the sky from the grassy knoll of the High Graffa, 'Has all England gone craven?' We had swords of peeled hazel and helmets of folded paper and when we hid motionless in the loft of the barn the ones who milked the cows below us were the Roundheads, and they would hang, draw and quarter us if we made a sound.

Pat, our older brother, read us *Robin Hood* and *Treasure Island* and *Hereward the Wake,* and we learned new dangers and lived new lives in the cart-house and the turf-shed and atop the bench of straw in the haggard. Our fantasies were filled with new faces and we had our image of them in our heads only: Blind Pew tap-tapping to the door of the inn and Little John and Hereward the Saxon king. We fought with the longbow and the quarterstaff and the cutlass. We hid a tin of bottle tops, i.e. doubloons, in the Páirc Bheags and drew a map and hid it in a bottle in the wall plate of the cart-house. We never went back to find them.

Books came in parcels from my Uncle Rick in America. He was a brother of my father's, and we knew nothing about him. We had never seen him, but we knew that his uncle, also called Richard, had worked with the *Chicago Tribune*. As soon as I could read, I devoured those books. In the days of summer, I longed for the deluge of rain that would come sweeping in over the Maamturk Mountains so that we would get a respite from the beet field or the dusty drudgery of hay, and I could read *Uncle Tom's Cabin* and *Kidnapped* and *The Swiss Family Robinson* and anything else that came my way. There were some books that were hidden, but I usually found them anyway. There was one called *Something Nasty in the Woodshed,* and I don't know why they hid it, because it was only a detective story about a body that was found in the woodshed. Maybe the title conjured up something a bit spicier in my mother's mind.

We read books about life in English boarding schools, like *Tom Brown's Schooldays* and *Ashwood to the Rescue,* and we learned about tuck-boxes and detention and pillow-fights and cricket. We even tried to play the game ourselves, with made-up rules and home-made hurleys and three scollops stuck in the ground.

My father read at every opportunity, sitting in the big Windsor chair in the arch of the fireplace, under the oil lamp, or by the front window in the days of drumming rain. He read the *Irish Press* and cursed roundly if someone brought him the *Irish Independent,* which he condemned, for reasons we found hard to understand at the time. He did not really like the newspapers, and he didn't like politics. He preferred books. He read the books of Maurice Walsh – *Black-cock's Feather, The Key Above the Door* and *The Road to Nowhere* – but his favourite author of all time was Zane Grey. He read all his books, over and over, and then we read them, and learned new words like 'mesa' and 'gulch' that made us feel as if we were much smarter than our friends when we played cowboys behind the rocks in Poll na Brafa.

My mother read religious magazines like the *Messenger of the Sacred Heart* and the *Far East.* They came into the house because she subscribed to them and she felt she had a duty to read them. I used to watch her as she read them with a quiet reverence, sitting in the hob by the fire on a quiet Sunday afternoon, the smell of fresh-baked bread emanating from the oven on the hearth beside her. She would nod in half-sleep, her tired, veined eyelids flickering over an old dream, and I would wonder if there was a sadness she did not share with anybody.

There were magazines besides religious ones. There

was *Old Moore's Almanac,* which we pronounced 'orminik' and which had the dates of the fairs and markets for all the country and predictions for storms and catastrophes of all kinds. There was a magazine that came from America called the *Country Gentleman* which had pictures of fox-hunting and showjumping and which my father hid if anybody was coming to visit because he thought it was a bit pretentious.

I remember one magazine especially that burst upon my callow consciousness like an opening flower. It was called *Wide World,* and every time I think of it I see a hunter levelling a gun at a charging lion in the jungle or a mountaineer hanging from a precipice. It was a magazine of true tales of adventure that had happened all over the wide world. On the frontispiece was a map of the world, with an arrow pointing out the precise place where each adventure occurred. That book taught me geography and history and above all it made me a witness to a world beyond my own, a world that I longed to know and explore and conquer.

Reading these books and magazines seemed to fill us boys with indescribable, explosive energy. We ran into the fields and through the lanes and over the walls as if we had been charged with a potent drug. Our minds raced ahead of our bodies; the years ahead of us could not possibly arrive in time. We had worlds to conquer and we couldn't wait.

Little did we know then that there would come a time when that simple world, so full of promise, would wane and fade and become a heavier place that would weigh us down with regret. I remember visiting home in the days before my father's final illness and seeing him sitting in the Windsor chair by the window, reading for the umpteenth time a large-print version of *The Lone Star Ranger*. The farm that he had nurtured and which had nurtured us in turn was growing wild around him. All his sons were gone and all his energy was gone with them. Beyond the window the field was thick with docks and thistles. The outhouses were falling down in the yard and the haggard was tenantless of corn-stacks. My mother bought all the groceries, including butter and milk and eggs and potatoes, from the travelling shop that called once a week. She gave her old-age pension cheque and got the groceries and change, and bent over now with rheumatism, carried them into the half-empty house. When she died, her bedroom was full of religious magazines and there were dozens of letters of both supplication and gratitude for subscriptions received from her for the missions in Africa and China and Latin America.

She had her own idea of the wide world and how to conquer it.

The Farmyard

When I was about four or five years old I was able to open the back door and step over the sheaf of straw and look out at the glass wall. It was not made of glass, but it was a high thick wall with lots of spaces between the stones where my mother would carefully lodge all the bits of broken jars and bottles and delft that were the casualties of the kitchen. The wall joined the gable end of the house and the other end formed the pier of the gate into the haggard.

One morning I heard a terrible squawking and flapping beyond the glass wall and I ventured warily to the gate to investigate. My mother was at the wooden chopping block. She had a small hatchet in one hand and the legs of a dangling red hen in the other. She had just chopped off its head, and as the hen danced its last gory dance blood spewed and spattered everywhere, all over the ground and my mother's crossover bib. Mother's face was averted, her eyes were half-closed and she blew gently through pursed lips as the life in her hands gradually ebbed away. I stood at the haggard gate, one foot on the bar, and watched the wild feathery flapping become a quiver, and then my mother looked up and saw me. 'There's your hag-hen now,' she said, her grin of disgust becoming a warm smile and her gentle eyes full of promise. I wanted to run and hug her and rub my child-cheek against the pearly skin of her neck. I would have liked to wash away the blood and all things threatening to her kindly nature and take her by the hand to some haven of rest, for she had opened the gates of my childhood prison and released me into the world of sky and sun. She was my liberator then, my destroyer of fears, standing there in her blood-spattered apron with the hatchet in her hand like some Celtic champion of old. Her image is thus to me, bright as ever in my memory still.

The farmyard was indeed a new world, a cobbled quadrangle of wheels and hooves, of horses being backed between the shafts of carts, of shiny leather harness and buckles and chains and calves peering with milky eyes from the dusky darkness beyond half doors. It was a world that woke in the bright morning to the lowing of cows and the whinnying and kicking of the horses from the stable and the quack of ducks and the crowing of cocks and the grunting of pigs and all the cacophony of things craving food and release. Food was on the way: hay walked on human legs across the yard, and buckets of sliced mangolds, and basins of scalded mash. There in the cow byre the row of cows munched, their lolling tongues dripping and their bulging eyes rolling in languorous ecstasy. All of a sudden I was a cocky explorer, my fear of living things gone forever.

I learned how to release the cows' chains and send them waddling in full-bellied line out across the yard and into the green fields beyond. I watched their pungent dung being swept up and tossed out through the hatch into the steaming dung heap, all mixed with straw that would rot and settle and be the underworld of worms and flies and blue backed beetles. There it would settle under the warm heat of the sun into a solid bank of energy, free from all things foreign, rich as rolled tobacco, fresh food for the hungry fields. It would be spread by the cartload in spring, to be washed down by the soft rains of April, coaxing up the verdant green sward of summer.

The brittle bedding straw was cut with a hay knife from the rick in the haggard and spread in the byre so the cows slept clean every night, warm and placid in their clanking chains, while the rain drummed on the iron roof overhead and the swallows twittered in the rafters.

Freed from my own chains of fear, I loved to lift the latch of the henhouse in the mornings and fill the air with feathered flight and raucous cackle as the red and white and brown birds all burst into brightness. Sometimes I would have to rouse the sleepy ones, still crouched in hooded sleep, getting too old and tired for this eternal struggle. I watched my mother call them round her in the yard, scattering rolled oats and meal as they strutted and scrapped at her feet. I learned to search in the currant bushes and in the straw and the nettle banks to where the adventurous among them wandered, and finding brown eggs in the latticed nests was like finding a hidden hoard of treasure. I would be rewarded with a slice of homemade madeira cake or a buttered scone.

The farmyard was the centre of the world then, a place where all things met and were sorted, a menagerie of moving life, an arena of animals and man and fowl and dogs and cats where everything should have been confusion but was not. There seemed to be an old order stamped by time, a hierarchy of beings, each with its own right of passage, each following a preordained path to its own destiny. The calves had their sheltered shed cut into the Graffa hill. There was the long low open turf shed, always three-quarters full, stacked meticulously at the open ends, row by row, sod by hand-laid sod, rain spilling under the dripping galvanize. There was room for the turnip slicer, and a little crib for a sick lamb. The horse had his own cobbled stable with his high, boarded manger and an iron pot set in concrete in the corner for his bran and rolled oats. It was a stable full of pent-up energy, where hooves flew in snorting frustration. He wanted to be kicking his heels in the freedom of fields. He would turn his head from the halter, fight the traces, rear up and buck under the threat of shafts or swingle. I would watch the battle between man and beast from the safety of the cart house. There was always a fireside tale of a man who was killed by a single kick of a horse; laid out stone cold with one black mark on his temple.

There was an August morning when, in the full hectic dust-filled flurry of hay being brought into the field beside the house and a sheep-cock being shaped round a pole, I sat, in my childish glee, in the empty horse cart, my legs dangling at the horse's side. I had ridden the bouncing cart to the meadow and back on top of the high swaying load of hay, sweeping under the hawthorn branches by the boreen, high as the gable of the house. Now I was ready for the next jaunt. Then, suddenly, there was the buzzing of a wasp, a frightened shaking of the horse's head, and then she jumped and bucked and I was gripping the cart until my father threw down his hayfork and swept me into his arms and the horse and cart careered off in a wild crazy driverless gallop round the field, men chasing and shouting and swearing and waving their coats. The horse made for the gap in the wall, missed the middle, the wheel hit the giall of the gap and the cart turned completely over, the horse on his back, hooves flailing, steel-rimmed wheels spinning in the air. I looked at that crushed space in the stony gap where I should have been, trapped under board and iron, and I clung to my father's sweaty, collarless, striped shirt and felt the once – and seldom repeated – warmth of his protection and love.

The Man of the House

When I was a child my father filled the frame of my vision, big and tall and strong as a stallion. His force and raging, pent-up energy filled the house like a storm. His days raced empty ahead of him and he bore down on them with relentless determination so that he would fill them with work. Black clouds lurked behind the mountains of his horizons, threatening devastating destruction of his precious crops. We had to race before the winds that bore them, getting the hay piled and weighted down with rope and stone, cutting the corn before the rains came to flatten it. He would seize on a dry gap in the day, a space between laden clouds when the sun shafted golden down on the heavy-headed oats and held it upright long enough for the swish of his scythe to save it. And in that summer of our lives, we would be with him in the corner of the cornfield, feeling his urgency, watching his stooping back move with the rhythm of his strokes and the sweat show through his striped shirt. We would take and tie and stand the sheaves, all slanted in rows of wigwam stooks. And the insides of our arms would cry out to us, stung and red and burnt with hidden nettle and thorns, but we would all be bound together in one purpose like the sheaves we harvested.

There was no time of the year when this great race with nature slackened. When the sun at Easter began to change the whitened ryegrass green, there would be ploughs to shoulder onto carts and wide-eyed horses to be buckled and tamed again for work. And there would be all the grunting sounds of turning the team of man and beast and plough at the headland and the bottle of tea swallowed hastily under the shelter of the thorn bush while the wind whistled between the stones in the wall behind him.

The first whitening of the fields with hoar frost in late October set his heart in a panic, with the potatoes still in the cold ground and the sugar beet to be pulled and crowned and stacked and carted onto the roadside. Then there were turnips and mangolds to be harvested and the stacks of corn to be thatched and made secure for the winter's raging. And all would be a-rushing and a-running with buckets and carts and a-rooping with aching fingers in the wet earth for the precious roundness of the nuggets, all hidden until this last prospecting tussle with the earth. Dried stalks gathered up to shield them from the winter snow, armfuls of straw to keep them warm, and clay again piled on them in a long, prism-shaped pit beside the house.

The sugar-beet harvest was a sustained attack over a week. There would be the order from the factory in Tuam, then the sharpening of beet knives that we would swing like machetes, lopping off the green leaves. The men would crown the beet, not trusting our aim with the blades. The beet-crowns would be winter fodder for the cows. The clay would have winter stickiness to it now, and the freezing fog would be lurking in the black trees. Our hands would be numb with the cold, our noses dripping, our boots lead weights, the roads where the carts crossed brown as a chimney. We would have the pile of beet by the road just in time for the lorry to come and bring it laboriously up the hill and away so that we could breathe again, knowing that in return there would be a cheque from Comhlucht Siúcra Éireann and a great big bale of sweet pulp for the sheep in winter.

Because my grandfather's name was Paddy, my father was known as 'Mick Phaddy', to distinguish him from all the other Walshes in the village. The name sat uneasily on his shoulders, because it also meant that he was 'faddy' – that he had a fad about things, that he was particular and temperamental and eccentric even – and that label was a little too close for comfort.

My father fought all his working life to be first, to be cleanest, to be tidier than anyone else. He wanted his house and his farm and his children to be admired and praised above others. He was competitive and proud and stubborn. His collar had to be starched on Sunday, the drills in his fields had to be straight, and the stooks of corn had to be in neat, even rows. There would be no breached walls to be seen on our land, no thistles or docks in the fields, no yellow *bráiste* in the oats. These were the needs that drove him: the need to be respected and admired and looked up to.

For him, the ways of farming were the old ways, ways that matched perfectly the ebb and flow of Mother Earth, ways and places marked by knowledge and fable and myth passed on by old people in the chimney corner. There were fields where certain crops flourished and fields that should never be broken and places that were cursed. He liked to do what his father before him had done, in the same way that he had done it. Tractors only messed up fields and dragged up hidden rocks in the ground that should never have been disturbed. Combine harvesters broke up the corn and left too much of a stubble.

He spoke reverently about the Balfour Act and the Ashbourne Act that had, not all that long ago, won for him on this small farm a security of tenure that his forebears had never known. He did not have to walk very far to find the ruins of the hamlet where people had lain down and died during the Famine, their mouths green with grass and nettles. There was no such thing as money to spare. There was an Economic War with Britain, and then there was compulsory tillage. The prospect of hunger and poverty was real. But there were many days of drudgery and hardship when he railed against the slavery of it all and cursed the big farmers who had 'a farm of land in every field' and did not appreciate it.

For my father, strength, agility and athleticism were gods. When he was twenty years old, big and strong as an ox, he was teased into a foolish bet at the crossroads outside Toole's shop on a Sunday. There was a huge round boulder there on the green, and it was said that nobody could ever lift it. He stooped and grappled and grabbed it between his arms and knees and lifted it clean as a whistle, but his back paid the price, for it was never right afterwards.

In those wild, bludgeoning days of his youth, he played a kind of Gaelic football that was more akin to the physical jousts of Fionn Mac Cumhaill and the Fianna. There was a local team called the Corrib Shamrocks: all farmers who played in hobnail boots – men like Welshman from Ballyhale and Jakes from Carheens and Pat Frank from over the road.

My father liked to talk of 'flattening somebody with a shoulder', or the day they played the university students from Galway. The students had come down in the steamer from the city, thin, pale-faced youths full of skill and speed, all weak as flowers in the shade of a wall. They played in Cargin, in a bumpy field over-looking the lake, and when fog descended halfway through the match, all hell broke loose. The locals were tired of getting the run-around and they started a free-for-all. The poor students never knew that football could be like that: raw and untamed as the jungle. They just about survived, and they all retired to the Ferry for porter afterwards, where there was song and laughter and talk of a rematch that everybody knew in their heart of hearts would never take place.

My father liked to take a drink, but he seldom had money to buy one. If he had a half-crown on a Sunday evening, he would walk to Headford with his friend Patrick Molloy the blacksmith and they would have two pints of porter each in the ticking quietness of Ryder's pub, a tiny length of wooden counter where nothing moved except the hands of the clock, where conversation was as slow as the imperceptible turning of the earth, and where men who knew each other and each other's families sat and mused on the weather and the price of sheep. In their talk and quiet dreaming, they turned over the uneventful days of their lives and stepped carefully around each other's sensitivities as if they were crossing a deep river on slippery stones.

As the night slipped slowly by and the sky framed by the small window gradually changed from blue to black, they eased into a state of mild contentment for a while, counting their blessings, recounting someone else's woes. The sweet, luxurious smell of porter, the hanging haze from the cigarettes they exchanged, the rows of shiny bottles on the shelves and the smoothness of the polished counter under their elbows was their paradise for one sweet time on earth.

They would walk home in the silvery moonlight, their strong shoes grinding the sand beneath their studied assuredness. Each had his own signature on the landscape that they crossed; each had his own reason for walking proudly, head high, under the moon. As they passed by our fields, the sculptured shapes of meadow cocks would stand to attention, clean and crisp as a row of apples in a stall. The wrought-iron gate at the head of our boreen would be a testimony to the craft of the other man, its whorls and twists shaped out of sweat and invention and an art dedicated to his friend.

My mother feared drink as the enemy of peace and

as the essence of all that was evil in the world. She preached against it, denounced it, and whenever she got the opportunity, she pointed out examples of those it had undone. Drink was the great monster that lurked under the ground our predecessors had trodden. Father Matthew had saved us. The Pioneer Association would guard us from its terrible excesses. We wore the badge and took the Confirmation pledge to abstain from alcohol until the age of twenty-one, and we did it publicly from the altar so that there would be no doubt about it.

Very rarely did my father get the chance to over-indulge himself in drink, but when he did, the door was unlocked on all the demons, and they rode roughshod over the quietness of our house. The temptation to stray came from an unexpected quarter.

At Christmas time and Easter, and again at harvest, there was a church collection. Master Garvey – the local headmaster – and my father were the collectors who sat in the church porch, gathering the pound notes and the ten-shilling notes and the half-crowns and writing the names in the priest's passbook. Father O'Grady, the parish priest, who roundly condemned from the altar all self-indulgence and drunkenness, always brought both his collectors into his house after the Masses and treated them to great big glasses of whiskey. If my father was late home for Sunday lunch, my mother feared the worse. Whiskey was something he was not used to. It stirred the aggressive demons in his soul and made him as wild and belligerent as a bull. There was such a Sunday deep in September, the long toil of corn easing into a kind of quiet respite with the shortening of the days. Time, surely, for some rest. My mother sat by the front window, fidgeting and watching the clock, twisting her apron and warning us not to provoke him if he came home fiery and full of goading mischief.

When he came rollicking home he started to play with us in the house. The play became rough-and-tumble, and then all hell broke loose: suddenly he lost his temper and my mother said in desperation, 'I told you all to stay away from him', and that was like a red rag to a bull for him and he banged the door on his way out to the yard and saddled the horse with a flurry of kicking hooves and bucking and yanking of the reins. He galloped off down the boreen and back the road at breakneck speed and over the hill at Cullen's and the sound of the iron on the road rang behind him.

How long he stayed away or where he went I don't know, but we were all sent silently to bed under the shadowy scraws though it was early and we had only time to swallow a meagre morsel of a supper. And we rested light-faced on our sheets and feared the worst. And nightmares rode on horseback through our dreams, riders with hollow bony eyes and black cloaks flowing in the wind over the graves of the dead. All was wailing and weeping for someone lost, someone drowned in a bog, someone swallowed up by the black waters of the lake or run through by the horns of a bull in a field.

When we got up in the morning, our father was already in the fields, and we were called to go and help him. We trooped out silently to the beet-field, where he stood among the green palmy leaves, bending and weeding, and we rowed in without a word, and eventually words did come slowly between us like a dreaming bird waking to song in the morning, and gradually and uneasily we settled into another day under the wide sky. My mother and father spoke politely to each other at the table when we ate, and soon, with the passing of that day and each day, the incident was forgotten and then nobody mentioned it ever again.

There was a winter day with frost white on the banks by the road and Christmas round the corner when he had to go into the village to cash the beet cheque and to collect a parcel from the bus. My father was gone a long time, and my mother was going to the window and looking at the flat winter sky as it darkened and filled in over the hill at Garraí Sheáin Seoighe. He should not be this long. He would have all that money. Who would he meet, that would tempt him into Varley's, and maybe he would spend all the money, and what would we do then? And she could not help thinking her black thoughts out loud and they took over her mind and ours, and the whole house became a wake-house with the darkening evening. Charlie was sent in to find him, though we all knew that this was a last resort: you did not insult a man by implying that he could not find his way home on his own, that he could not be trusted.

We were huddled in our beds above the kitchen

much later that night when he came talking in, loud in his hushed whispers, mellow and silver-tongued and staggering against the chairs and saying, 'Sing us a song, Annie, go on, sing us a song, just for me. Sing "The Roses" for me in your sweet voice.' And he was hustled to bed carefully, so that the dam of his temper did not break.

Sleep soon rescued him and would rescue us as always, and we smiled on our pillows that the pillar of the house was still standing and that the silent darkness that reached up to enfold us held no threat after all.

Fair days were days when drink could drive men crazy; you had to be careful. There was suddenly money in the hand, and friends at your shoulder, and cosy nooks in pubs with glistening rows of bottles and polished glasses and long draughts of beer that was like honey on the tongue. In there, with the full kick of tobacco in your lungs and the pop and swirl from the neck of a whiskey bottle, you could forget the stony ground that jolted the plough, and the lambs that died in the snow, and the demands of women. As you vainly tried to make your light-headed way up to the top of the town, there were calls from different friends and neighbours to 'have a small one for the road home', and you could not refuse an offer from your cousin, or the man who lent you the scuffler, or Pat Frank who played football in Cargin with you against the students.

But my father was able to tread carefully through these minefields and usually arrived home safe and high-spirited, having sold the lambs for a record price and bought calves that were the best bargain at the fair. But most of all, in our young and innocent eyes, there was a fair day when he covered himself in glory and brought home a bounty that made him forever a hero. It was the October fair, the end of the toil of summer and harvest, the selling of the fruits of labour, the easing into an already provided-for winter. He arrived home with the carrier piled high with boxes tied with twine and wrapped in the cleanest brown paper we had ever seen. We gathered round that stone-floored kitchen like orphans at a picnic, wide-eyed and wondering at the gifts about to be bestowed. The lids opened to reveal gleaming leather boots, leather thongs in the riveted eyes, and rows of shiny hobnails around the soles. Oh great kicking heaven, what thundering days were ahead, what sliding on the ice of the turlough, what dryness in the flood, what safety under the stomping of man and beast! These were the badge of manhood, the weapons of war, the clink of iron on stone. They would hold us up from the gutter – fill our hearts with pride and the hearts of our enemies with fear. With boots like these, we could safely hunt the wild badger in the shore and the lurking rat in the stable; we would be safe and dry and warm and loved forever.

The brown paper was spread on the floor so that we could fit on the boots and they would be returnable if they were the wrong size. No boots were ever returned. We could not bear the thought. Once they were laced in place round our ankles, we would not part with them for our lives. Though my mother pressed the toecaps and felt for space for growth, and made us walk along the path of brown paper and pondered the size and the fit, we were, in our own minds, already suited in our armour, tall as the house, ready to dash to freedom through the open door. I scrunched up my toes to make sure that her probing thumb would find ample room under the leather. My toes have been crippled ever since, but what were a few cramped toes compared to freedom and confidence and pride? My father was a hero and I was about to become one, and my brothers and I, in our new leather boots, would conquer the world.

A PRIEST IN THE FAMILY

My brother Charlie was the eldest of the family. He was nineteen years older than me. He would have been a farmer like my Dad, but he was very clever at school and got a scholarship funded by the Jesuits to St Ignatius College in Galway. He stayed in my Aunt Nora's house in Shantalla, and though she had a large family of her own, she looked after him for the five years he spent at school. Then he announced that he was going to be a priest. He left for the seminary in Carlow two months before I was born, but he came home on holidays, dressed all in black. He was a joker. He dressed me up in my mother's hat and coat and took my photograph sitting on the wall between two pots of geraniums. He frightened us so badly with stories about the 'Small Window Ghost' that was supposed to appear on the landing window that we were afraid to close our eyes at night. He teased us about everything and set us fighting among each other. He organised games where we unwittingly made fools of ourselves. But behind it all he had a serious and studious nature. He was the apple of my mother's eye, her bright and shining star.

It was a great honour to have a priest in the family. There were many young men studying for the priesthood at that time, preparing for the foreign missions in China and Africa and South America. There wasn't a black speck appearing in the distance of a white summer road but would turn out to be a soutaned seminarian, slowly walking and reading his office – Latin words sometimes audible behind the wall of a field by the road: *'Bone pastor panis vere . . . '*

Mothers prayed silently and long that their sons would persevere at the seminary, that they would not fail, that they would not give in to the ways of the world. A young man who fell by the wayside was known as a spoiled priest, a man without a purpose in life. People did not know what to say to such a man. What could they say? How could they console him?

There was a great celebration for Charlie's ordination and First Mass. Strings of green laurel stretched across the roads. Bonfires burned at every crossroads and wisps of straw were placed at the gate of every neighbour's house. Our house teemed with young men in black, their cassocks flapping around their ankles, my mother smiling and misty-eyed, locals with tanned necks kneeling to be blessed by a white hand in cruciform signal over their bowed heads, money pressed into protesting palms for a Mass offering, a special intention. For a while the house and yard became a place of pilgrimage, a kind of shrine where well-dressed people came even on weekdays, when we should be at the hay. Men dressed in Sunday suits, women with hats that had a net to cover the eyes, eyes that hid jealousy and admiration and despair. There was tea in abundance, and ham and tomatoes, and white tablecloths and china cups. There was marble cake and seed cake and Madeira cake and the odd glass of sherry, but nothing stronger. There were plenty of banishments of us younger ones to the scullery, and strange cars in the yard, where we sat in and smelt the leather upholstery and imagined long journeys to the ends of the earth.

It was my mother's finest hour, her golden era of summer. But it was always haunted by the darkness of imminent parting, which loomed like a black cloud on the horizon, the cold wind of sadness blowing it ever nearer. The days grew quiet with the gloaming and talk became leaden in the evenings when the last visitor had closed the door behind him. My mother starching and sorting clothes, the smoothing iron always on the coals and the pile of suits and vestments in the big trunk growing higher and higher. My mother alternately cried and chastised herself for being selfish in the sight of God. My father sat in his Windsor chair twisting his cap and looking out at the red sun setting far in the west, towards the great prairies of America, where his eldest son was going soon. Maybe it would be like his two sisters, Katy and Margaret, who had left for America in 1925, never to return. He remembered the American wake, as they so aptly called the farewell party: the fiddle music and the dancing – all that forced joy. He remembered the small pier in Kilbeg, where the steamer that plied Lough Corrib stole them away in a flurry of steam and churning water. For the old people of the house, it was like giving up your children to death, shutting yourself away from them, half the world away, never again to hear the sound of their voices, or feel the touch of their hands, or catch a glimpse into their eyes. The only cord that would connect them now, from three thousand miles away where they lived with strangers, would be words traced in ink on a page.

The dreaded day dawned. The trunk and cases piled and tied into the open boot of Tom Moran's big black Plymouth. Neither of my parents would go to Cobh to see him board the liner. They would say their goodbyes here by the gable of the house. This is how he would remember their faces, their hunched forms in the shadow of the hawthorns. He would not have to pick them out from a sea of faces. Their white handkerchief would be the last focus through the mist of tears as the overloaded car chugged up Carrowbeg Hill.

I was only six years old, but I was able to climb the copper beech and watch the car disappear over the hill. I wondered why they were going east, towards the town, when Father Charlie had told me that America was over there to the west, beyond the Connemara Mountains and wild green ocean waves rolling.

The Parlour

The parlour was a place apart from all the flurry of farm work and the noisy turmoil of the child-mad kitchen. The low parlour door beside the arch of the kitchen was kept shut from everyday commonness. Inside was a kind of shrine to all aspirations and illusions of grandeur. There was linoleum on the floor, an old mahogany table, lace curtains on the window, papered walls and ceiling and a big black ornate china cabinet. Under the window there was a small bamboo table with an onyx top, and on it was a big stuffed pheasant with shiny plumage and long black tail, its black eye bright as a button, its claws fixed firmly on a mossy rock.

In the far corner of the room stood a delicate whatnot, also made of bamboo, and its shelves held a smooth and varnished seashell, a china figurine. There was a wrought-iron fireplace with a mantelpiece that had an American clock and two bronze figures on either side, one of a proud man with a hat sowing seed, and the other of a woman in a bonnet binding a sheaf of corn. While they worked, they seemed to look at each other, over the clock. I never knew where they came from, and nobody ever told me, but to my young eyes then, and ever since, when those upright idealistic figures flicker in the memory, they are the solid representations of my mother and father – how they would have seen themselves in whispered promises, their young hearts full of hope. He would sow and she would reap the fruits of their toil and they would look lovingly at each other forever across the ticking arm of time.

Here were shadows of a different kind from the turbulent shadows of the kitchen, shadows of a Sunday evening, the low red sky in the window-pane, my mother in her white blouse with the mother-of-pearl buttons, fingering old faded photographs, her calloused thumb rubbing the dust away, her eyes quiet and deep and limpid as a pool.

They were sepia-coloured photographs of moustachioed men in hard hats and long coats, and stately women with billowing black dresses and lace mantillas. The lady would always be seated, the man standing behind her, a hand on her shoulder. There were photographs of picnics and parasols on the lawns of stately homes beside the lake, and somewhere between the stiff pages of an album there was a crocheted doily, mysteriously and delicately wrapped in tissue paper.

A green oil lamp with a round glass globe, too delicate ever to be used, stood on the china cabinet, which shone with little mirrors and whirling pointed poles. This was a casket of Christmas smells, a little lock on the door guarding the odd bowl of setting jelly or bottle of raspberry cordial. The parlour was, in fact, a Christmas room, reserved for festivals, for Station breakfasts when the parish priest sat to a white linen cloth on the table and tea from a china cup. For most of the year the small iron fireplace lay dormant, but on frosty Christmas mornings my mother would fill the fire-shovel with red coals from the kitchen and scurry, smoke-trailed, into that cold room. The unused chimney would belch and cough and protest and we would hold a double sheet of newspaper tight against the grate, letting the draught roar, and sometimes the tempted paper would erupt in flames and the black, red-fringed fragments would go dancing round the room, threatening conflagration.

My father feared wind and fire in equal measure, his nightmares riding on tales of the Big Wind of 1829, the year before the house was built, when the rampant gales blew down chimneys, scattering the fire on the hearth, and the tinder-dry thatched houses whooshed into flame. For that reason, our house had been built in a hollow dug out of the shoulder of the High Graffa, a sweeping hillock of a field that was itself low down in the shelter of the green valley of Carrabeg.

He told us how the men with spades dug the scraws of turf and laid them aside for the roof, how they drew the big limestone rocks to that place in drays and carts, built the walls and gable thick as the length of a man's arm, cut the rafters from the rough hawthorn trees and worked a web of sally rods between to support the sods of earth and the thatch over that. They built the whole house in a week. They were not only builders but also neighbours, gathered with spades and hatchets and billhooks to set a couple in shelter, to rescue them from the wind and rain. When we lay on our beds, we looked up at the slanting lattice of sticks and dried scraws. We thought of the men in hard hats and collarless shirts who had encased us, and we tried to see their faces in the blackened landscape that sighed and creaked above us. In our sleepy imaginations, they smiled down on us, these village builders of the house we slept in. They had created a dry living space within which life could bloom and blossom, and that was enough for them on that week in their lives.

The couple whose house they built were my great-grandparents, who had come from the other end of the village where the little houses were on top of each other. The house brought them good fortune. When, in 1847, fever and famine swept through the cluttered hamlet they had left behind, they survived in the open space here beside the road. The families who had gathered together to heave the gable of their shelter into place had themselves been decimated, and their own little hovels one by one crumbled into silent ruin.

My great-grandfather, by all accounts, became silent too. Like the sole survivor of a holocaust, he turned in on himself and struggled between gratitude and bitterness. His son, my grandfather, who died two years before I was born, inherited his father's irascibility. In his last years, he was fractious and sharp as a nettle, sitting by the fireside and finding fault with every-body's way of doing things.

His photograph is here too, standing on the top of the china cabinet, looking down now on an ordered world that he helped rescue from the jaws of destruction.

THE SEPARATOR

Beyond the cross door with its wooden bolt was the scullery, where we were sometimes hunted if visitors came in or if the noise level became intolerable in the kitchen: 'Get out to the scullery!' It was like being banished to a penal colony. The scullery was a long, galvanized lean-to at the back of the house – a kind of back kitchen with a little window overlooking the farmyard. There was a small dairy at one end and the back door to the yard at the other. The scullery sheltered the house from the sharp east wind in winter, and on summer mornings the shafts of yellow sun shone through the rising steam and the dust motes that danced up from the stone floor.

It was a moist, steam-filled, bustling place, where the raw fragrance of the fields fought and mingled with the smell of cooked food and the strong smell of soap. You could smell raw cabbage, turnips, fried onions and boiled potatoes all at the same time, and sometimes there might hang slyly in the air the faint, sweet, pungent whiff of cows from the byre. No smell would surprise you, for this was a railway station of a place, buckets of fresh water brought in from the well, a pot of boiled potatoes being strained, clothes being scrubbed on the washboard, somebody carrying milk through to the dairy, men clumping through in their hobnail boots from the field. There was a washstand with a chipped basin, along with washboards and scrubbing brushes and packets of washing soda and starch. A red geranium fought for survival in the window and a hunched white cat looked in from his perch on the sunny windowsill outside.

You might lift a stray cabbage leaf and an earwig would go scurrying across the stone floor. *'Dearg a'Diabhail'* we called him: the devil's red friend. He was hard to kill. He seemed to survive our grinding boot-heels and could crawl to safety even if we had split him in two. He, too, plagued our nightmares, and in the darkness we hid beneath the blankets for fear of him dropping from the scraw roof above us into our open-mouthed sleep. But the scullery was swept clean a million times a day: there was a sheaf of straw at the door where you wiped your clay-clogged boots, the cabbage was washed and rinsed in salted water, and there was ever a vigilant eye for all creeping invaders.

The dairy at the end of the scullery was a white-washed corner of clanking buckets and enamelled basins and pails, with the sweet smell of fresh milk from the byre and the sharper scent of buttermilk. There were wooden bowls and butter bats and a hooped churn with a big handle that we had to turn forever before we heard the clunk of butter and the swish of buttermilk inside. The butter came out in soft lumps of deep yellow and my mother would gather it in the wooden basin, where it was pressed and beaten with a wooden saucer into a golden, elliptical mound. Sometimes she would leave a small portion aside before salting the rest. Unsalted butter was a cure for burns and scalds and all irritations of the skin. It was also handy if you were stuck for something with which to grease the axle of a cart or the chain of a bicycle.

If there was a special occasion imminent, my mother would ply her butter-bats and with the turn of her wrist she would transform a lump of butter into small shapes, rippled whorls and coils and spirals, snails' houses and seashells and little spinning tops that looked like a pile of golden candy laid out on a glass dish. At times like this she sang: her creativity brought out the music in her, and she sang in a quiet, faint, melodious voice:

Donald came across the heather,
Shook a raindrop from the feather
Of his bonnet blue, his bonnet blue . . .

The butter prints that she fashioned were for visitors only; they were for occasions of polite conversation and china cups, when women discussed vague things with a rueful shaking of heads at the passing of politeness and civility.

The most tedious and time-consuming job in the dairy was separating the cream from the milk, skimming it delicately with a saucer. My mother would spend hours peering across the surface of the pail trying to trap the elusive nuggets of cream. My enigmatic father hated change. 'We'll do what we always did,' he would say emphatically whenever there was talk of new methods. But he also liked to be first in the neighbourhood with something new. So he came home one day, after selling cattle at the fair, with a white wooden crate in the back of the cart. It was carried in to the kitchen and broken open to reveal a hundred steel parts wrapped in oil-paper. We formed a circus ring of gaping wonder round it, my father the ringmaster of mysterious new things from the world of technology, answering no questions, only saying, 'Wait till you see, wait till you see.'

Finally, a green, wrought-iron machine was bolted to the edge of the dairy table. When you turned the handle, the mechanism whirred into life, turning a cone-shaped silver wheel on which were placed in precise sequence about ten stainless-steel, conical discs, with intricate holes and lips and apertures. There must have been twenty components to be slotted and screwed into place, but everything fitted together with the precision of a clock. Then a small spout was attached, then more disks, then a thicker spout and a big silver bowl on top. The steaming milk was poured into the bowl, the handle turned at a breakneck pace, and lo! out of the thin spout, skimmed milk poured into a waiting vessel, and out of the other spout came the cream, first in a trickle, then in a steady stream, into the bowl placed underneath. I thought – we all thought – that this was the most wondrous invention in the living world. 'If the old people were alive to see this, they'd bless themselves surely,' my father said, pushing his cap well back and scratching his head. Then he went out and left us to our new toy. We all claimed, even after only one demonstration, that we knew exactly how to put it together. We fought for the honour of being the chief engineer and operator, we listened to the centrifugal whirr of the hub and the clink of the slick gears as they notched into action and then we gazed in awesome wonder at the pouring spouts. Fresh milk divided as if by the rod of Moses into skimmed milk and cream, all at the turn of a handle. The skimmed milk was thin and clear, without a speck of wasted butter floating on its blue surface. The cream was thick and rich and molten. Somehow, there was a sense that a clinical, radical change had taken place in the old order of things. Who ever heard of pure skimmed milk before? How could there be the same nutrition in it? Things would never be the same. The calves would surely sense the change. The pigs were bound to grunt and snort their disapproval. The spinning hub of a new idea would throw their taste buds into confusion and they would live now, like ourselves, at the cutting edge of chaos.

JULIA

Julia was the youngest of my sisters, five years older than the twins, seven years older than me. She was God's creature, not man's. Nobody ever really spoke about, or tried to explain to the rest of us, why she was as she was: simple and guileless and fun-loving – the eternal mirror and reservoir of our childhood innocence. We grew up to recognize that she was special and exasperating and precious, but that realization only came to us as gradually – and as certainly – as the green fields turning brown.

There were dark nights when our sleep was disturbed by a commotion, and we half-overheard talk of fits and swallowing the tongue and holding it down with the end of a spoon. And there was the odd day when we saw what we were not meant to see: a convulsion, a foaming at the mouth, a holding-down and praying. But she was for us boys then a grown-up child, a big soft companion that knew nothing of the dark ways of the world. And in the gloaming of dewy summer evenings she and I were teachers who taught lessons to the nettles and lashed them senseless with a switch. At the glass wall, under the mottled shade of the whispering copper beech, we played shop with the old broken crockery and fragments of glass that all became commodities for sale. We prized bits of blue glass, old rusted tins, cigarette boxes. We made shelves from scraps of timber and our cash box was a biscuit tin. We had our currency of buttons and old washers, and the walls of the shop were lines drawn in the dust. And the most abiding thing I remember from those guiltless days was her wide-eyed laughter.

Sometimes we were the witches of the western world, digging a hole with our hands in the quietness of a hedge-held field, filling it with water from the stream, adding frogs and beetles and worms and mixing it into a murky potion that we would reserve for all the enemies of innocence. And at night before bedtime we were taught to pray that God would not take her from us, and we grew up to be at once her playmates and the protectors of her simple soul. If other boys jeered her, we fought them with our bare knuckles.

Julia was an epileptic. Epilepsy was a new word then, a condition about which very little was known. Our parents certainly did not talk about it, nor did visitors to the house. The question of heredity was very much in people's minds. Houses where TB was present were avoided as much as possible. People were proud and careful and discreet. They did not sweep things under the carpet, but they minded their own business, and their own families came first. If somebody sought their help, they were never slow to offer it. But they did not patronise people or publicise such business. There were certain things you kept to yourself and there were special burdens that you shouldered alone.

Julia never learned to read or write. She might have, if she had had special help. She was not dull, but the cogwheels of her mind were different from ours. She could remember the day and date of everybody's birthday, and their precise age, but she could not add or subtract. She could describe the dress that such a one wore to Mass on a certain Sunday, but she struggled to form the letters of the alphabet on the page. Teachers gave up on her; the classes were too big to give individual help. The rest of us tried to help her at home, but we hadn't got the patience. She got too excited when things did not come to her and she would stammer and then she would be left alone. Nobody wanted to run the risk of bringing on a fit or a convulsion. At that time there were no drugs or tablets to help her. So she eased into a dreamy state of being, among us and yet outside of us, her eyes reflecting another past and a different future, her actions moving to a rhythm that was set on another plane above and beyond our understanding.

She fitted into a role that was simple and straight-forward. She learned to milk the cows and go to the well for water and go to the shop with a list. But she could not handle money or count the change. She helped in the fields, but only with simple tasks like turning hay or picking potatoes.

What she loved was music, and dancing, and songs. She lived for Station parties and a chance to sing in her sweet, melodious, lilting voice, struggling to remember the words, relishing the applause and the attention that she craved. This was her way of life, uncomplicated by money or ambition or worries about the future. What mattered was that precious present moment when everybody sang and danced and laughed together, when pain and isolation were forgotten, when she felt for once that what she had to offer was important too. I remember one such twilight, and I can still hear her light, airy tones drifting round the old house. It was in the dying days of Station parties:

When the curtains of night are pinned back by
*   the stars,*
And the beautiful moon lights the sky,
And the dewdrops of heaven are kissing the rose,
It is then that my memory flies,

As if on the wings of a beautiful dove
In haste with the message it bears,
Just to bring you a kiss of affection and say:
'I'll remember you, love, in my prayers.'

When the heavenly angels are guarding the
*   good,*
As God has ordained them to do,
In answer to prayers I have offered to Him,
I know there is one watching you.

*And may its bright spirit be with you through
    life
To guide you up heaven's bright stairs,
And meet with the one who has loved you so
    true
And remembered you, love, in her prayers.*

'Good on you, Julia!' they all said. The song could have been her anthem. I know that there was a special bright spirit that guided her through life, and through all the loneliness and isolation that never conq148uered her, and I know that heaven's bright stairs will lead her straight through the golden gate.

Out into the Land of Plenty

With all those female guardians to keep me in the periphery of their vision as they scurried about their farm or household business, I ventured to explore outside that sleeping farmhouse, round the tiny walled front garden, beyond the giant copper beech that guarded the gable like a sentinel, and into the haggard, which for most of the year looked like a Turkish city, with its turreted stacks of corn, some raised high on stone trestles, all pointed skywards like a perpetual offering to the gods. These were my father's brood of bounty, bracing their rounded backs against all weather. The precious dry corn in their bone-dry centres whispered, 'Thou shalt not starve.' They were a testament to sweat in the fields and artistry of an ancient kind: tightly packed sheaves turned in rounded, ever-widening circles until you reached the *bunsop,* and then drawn gradually inwards to reach a pointed top. They were clipped and preened and thatched with rushes stitched with pointed hazel scollops and wrapped at the very top with hemp bags weighed down with stones that dangled from their wide bellies, making them look like Oriental dancers. They guarded their precious seed when the frozen ground of winter sang like iron and when the February rains cascaded onto them, sweeping in over the roof of the barn. You could stand under their slanting sides and be dry, and watch the needles of rain drip in steady streams round you, and feel that you were in some kind of silver cage.

Here, as a small boy, I watched wide-eyed the turmoil of threshing. What a wonder for a small boy! A great red-and-yellow monster hauled into the haggard by a belching blue tractor. Men suddenly everywhere, a maelstrom of flying straw and chaff, sheaves tossed and fed into the droning, churning, cavernous creature that bristled with moving belts and turning wheels and clattering noises from its mysterious insides. The great big Fordson Major tractor behind it, attached with a white twisted belt that sliced the air with menace. Everybody shouted warnings as they scurried by: 'Don't go near that or it will cut your head off!'

The wonder of it was that it could separate every-thing. My father stood on top of the stack, undoing its circled secrets, tossing the sheaves which he had once harboured to this relentless monster. Paddy Charlie cut the bands with a sharp knife as if he were slashing the throats of children, and then fed them into the roaring, gobbling mouth. It churned and munched and coughed out shuddering bundles of straw from its headless throat to where my brother Pat stood. He forked it up to Joe, Paddy Charlie's brother, who piled it into a huge rounded heap. Under the monster's mouth was a slit that belched out chaff that went flying on the wind and whirling all over the place like golden snow. At the tail-end of the wooden leviathan, Mickeen Charlie ministered with bags that he hung on hooks beneath four small chutes, out of which poured a steady stream of corn. He tasted it and chewed it and ran it through his fingers as if he were the counting clerk of a precious currency. He was a small black weasel of a man, always up to some trick. He went to the tractor and put his left hand into the engine and stretched his right hand towards me. 'Come here,' he called to me, 'and shake hands.' I didn't really want to, but I thought it impolite to refuse. When I touched his greasy fingers, an electric shock nearly jolted my arm from its socket. He laughed like a hyena. My brother explained that it was the dynamo, but I believed that Mickeen Charlie was some kind of evil spirit who wanted to hurt children. After that, I ran away from him whenever he came near.

When the tumult of threshing had died down and the great red-and-yellow monster had been hauled away, the haggard was a changed place, all robbed of its ordered shape, full of tumbledown straw and scattered chaff and standing stones topped by flat, empty flags. But my father always seemed to spare one stack of corn without sacrificing it to the devouring machine. It was as if he guarded against a future famine, some unforeseen disaster that might befall. Or sometimes there would be a stack of wheat kept for thatching the house. Straw broken and bent by the threshing machine was useless for thatching; it had to be slashed, by hand, in the barn.

The slashing stone stood sentinel outside the back door of the barn. Nothing we knew was as old as this stone. It was a great big rounded boulder, shiny as a plate, polished by the hefty strokes laid on it by those whose ghosts now prowled the fields. On it had fallen honest sweat; its convex surface mirrored pale, distorted forms that had carried on this same work since time began.

When the time came, it was lifted onto a horizontal ladder about three feet from the ground at one end of the barn. This was draped in empty sacking to make a counter, so that there was a narrow space between it and the wall, where the seed, flying and jumping from the flayed stems, would be trapped.

My father would strip to the waist, his white rippling muscles straining, lashing the polished rock with the bunched stalks. Shining in perspiration, he rained down blow upon blow, pausing breathless every now and then, hands resting on the stone, hunched over it, adding his dripping sweat in offering to the gods of history. It was killing work. The straw would then be teased and shaken out gently and tied in precious, neat sheaves. When the wind was right, the seed and chaff would be tossed in the air between the two doors of the barn, and the chaff would blow in a drift towards the back door and there would be seed on the black, polished flags of the floor.

Beyond the haggard was the orchard, with a little wooden gate and a latch that I, in my toddling explorations, struggled to reach, but that little gate opened onto a paradise of sweet smells and pink-and-white blossoms and tastes that startled our untutored tongues with ecstasy. It was a place where shafts of green light tumbled into small clearings, where the wind was tamed into a whisper, where the thud of an apple on the grass would startle you into thinking that there were spirits here of a special kind. A belt of larch and silver beech on the north and east sides sheltered the fruit trees so that no late winter wind would shake them. The apple trees were pruned into candelabra, with wide forks close to the ground that even a small boy could step up into. We perched up there for long hours of summer like birds brooding, letting the green sun filter through the sinewy leaves and watching the tiny spiders scurry and swing on their silky filaments. Sometimes we were trapped up there by the geese that prowled the waving grass for windfalls. Their sharp razor beaks were menacing. We would jump and run, and this would be followed by a beating of wings and a trumpeting, heart-thumping cacophony of yellow beaks.

There were giant green cookers in that land of plenty, and bitter crabs for making jelly, but there was one tree of sweet apples that were our blissful bounty. Beauty of Bath, we were told they were, and they were beauties of a kind to us never to be repeated, a red-and-orange-streaked hardness, a crunching, juicy sweetness on the innocent tongue of childhood. Like patient savages, we crouched, waiting in the grass for them to ripen, staring skyward to where they hung and swayed tantalisingly above us. Then, as if by ordination, a hazy July morning would bring a whiff of ripeness, a solemn pronouncement from somewhere above that the bountiful harvest was here at last. Before that feast of plenty, we would have been content with the gooseberries and blackcurrants that grew in tangled plenty beneath the trees. Their tartness furred our tongues – a poor prelude of what was to come. But we did our best to make them into a feast. We pinched the eyes out and laid them on a saucer, covered them with a ton of sugar and a few spoonfuls of cream stolen from the warm pail in the scullery, and had a dessert fit for kings. As with every seasonal profusion that opened to us, we would over-indulge; our stomachs would cramp up and then explode in liquid streams. We could defecate through the eye of a needle. Our mother said that it was good: it was a seasonal scouring and cleansing by Mother Nature.

NIGHT GAMES

On the long winter nights after the lamp was lit and the Rosary was said, we did our best to pass away the slow, ticking time. The radio brought Dick Barton and Perry Mason, but the wet battery seemed to be always low, and we were, more often than not, left to our own devices.

Whenever Charlie – he who in later life became vicar general of the diocese of Wichita, Kansas – was at home, we were never short of amusement. He ran things, even then. He would gather us all on the hearth while he stood imperiously in front of the fire, blocking the heat. He would anounce with great pomp that a 'Question Time' had been organised for eight o'clock and that we had better sharpen our wits or we would disgrace ourselves in front of everyone. He even had the audacity to look for an entrance fee of one half-penny from everyone, but had to abandon that tack when it was clear that nobody had any money.

The prizes had to be donated. Once, my brother Pat volunteered a prize that Michael, Jim and I really craved. It was a little tractor that he had made. He cut notches in a wooden spool and, with two small nails, a rubber strip cut from the tube of a bicycle, a lollipop stick and a piece of candle to eliminate friction, made a device that you could wind up and which crawled magically across the oilcloth from one side of the kitchen table to the other. Mind you, if you wound it too much, it jumped crazily out of control like a drunken jackrabbit. The girls were not too keen on the prize. Rose offered her slippers with the cardboard soles that she had got from Santa Claus as a prize, if the winner should be of the female gender.

Being the youngest, I got the easiest questions: 'How many jugs on the dresser?' 'How many hoops on the churn?' 'What is the name of Charlie Joe's dog?'

The twins, who were just two years older than me, got slightly trickier questions, like: 'How old is the cat?' or 'What's Pat Biddy Flynn's real name?'

The questions the girls got seemed to be based largely on *The New Progress Arithmetic* or Nesfield's *Outline of English Grammar:* 'If a cow and a calf eat a turnip and a half in a day and a half, how many would they eat in a week?' or 'What is the collective noun for partridge?'

Or 'Forty sheep went out a gap, forty more went after that, and the shepherd and his dog. How many legs went out the gap?' Somebody piped up: 'Charlie Joe's dog has only three legs.'

There was a row. There was always a row. I never remember anyone winning a prize.

Sometimes we played 'I Spy'. Michael, who was too young to play, shocked the whole assembly one night by spying something, he said, beginning with 'H'. When everybody had finally given up guessing, he pointed to the dog asleep beside the fire and said, 'Hoor'. Greeted with an incredulous, stunned silence, he explained that sometimes when my father was rounding up the sheep he would say to the dog: 'Get outside them, you hoor!'

There was a game we played called 'Naming Houses'. If it was your turn, you would say something like, 'Michael and Bridget on their own', and the rest of us were supposed to know that they were the Lees of Curramore. This was not as easy as it sounds. There were Michaels and Bridgets at every turn of the road, and they all had nicknames. We never knew them as Michael or Bridget anyway. They could be Michael Phádraig and his wife, or Michael and Biddy Earnor, or Bríd Bandy and her brother Mick. This game was just as contentious as 'Question Time'. We would argue and fight until my mother got tired of us and sent us to bed.

The silence of the dark space under the sloping thatch would be punctuated by scornful remarks and recriminations: 'You don't even know who the Lees in Curramore are.' 'Yes I do, and I know who Pat Biddy Flynn is, which is more than you do.'

My words and opinions carried little weight, so I just closed my eyes and dreamed of the time when I might glean enough knowledge out of the world around me to be able to win magical things like tiny wooden tractors powered by elastic bands, that could travel all the way from one end of the table to the other.

SCHOOL

School was the great adventure, the tearing away from ties. When I was four years old and top-heavy with a big head, I was bundled off to Claran National School. I had seen the building across the road from the church. It looked foreboding, grey upon grey, a dark hulk with iron railings and tall windows and dark green doors shut tight to hide the dreadful pain within.

'Wait until Mrs O'Kelly gets you,' my brothers and sisters said. That was a nice introduction. Nothing like a warning like that to make you feel at ease. I imagined her as a witch. In fact, I was right.

The school year started on the first of July. That was the day classes changed and new recruits came in from cluttered houses to gather, in fearful anticipation of Mrs O'Kelly's wrath, for she was the teacher of Low Babies and High Babies. Children got physically sick with fright at her shrill voice and violent temper. Their older sisters were made clean the sick up, or cover it with turf-mould from the shed. Little bundles clung to their mother's aprons at the gate of the school and had to be torn away and lifted into that gloomy prison, away from the freedom of fields and the slow ease of nature that had surrounded them. Tables and spellings and penmanship and Irish were beaten into them. They would remember her long after they had forgotten all she taught them, and they would not remember her with pleasure.

Mrs O'Kelly was a sadist. She pulled and twisted ears. She landed stinging blows on the faces of small country urchins for no apparent reason other than that she seemed to hate them. She put ribbons in boys' hair and made them stand in the corner to be mocked. She made children go out into the yard and pull a switch to be beaten with.

I knew something of what lay ahead as I walked in the middle of my brothers and sisters back up the road to school for the first time. My sisters held my hands, one on either side. My brothers ran back and forth ahead and behind, wild with excitement: 'Look what we have. A new Low Baby. Our Tommy's starting today.' Friends who had been on the road before us slowed down to join the show. Others caught up. I was the centre of attention, like a new animal caught for the zoo. The boys looked at me and said, 'You're in for it!' and mimed a severe whacking and wailing. The girls cooed and preened and said, 'Oh, isn't he lovely! He's such a dote! Mrs O'Kelly is going to love you.' But they said it in such a way that I felt like a new sacrifice, another lamb to the slaughter.

I was finally pushed in the door of the Low Babies room, and the ogre was there to greet me. She was tall and bony, and everything about her looked as if it had been honed to a sharp point. Her nose was hooked and her elbows stuck out of her short sleeves like the blades of a windmill. Her bony fingers were covered with golden rings and her nails were long and pointed as spurs. Her brassy hair was piled on her head in a single antler and she pranced about the room on high heels like a grey crow stalking a newborn lamb. I was scared to death from the start. So were all the other Low Babies. Even the High Babies, who peopled the far side of the room under the tall windows, seemed transfixed in fright, motionless and pale-faced, their eyes firmly fixed on her supreme being. Somebody wet the floor. She shook the child like a dog would shake a rabbit.

We were put into desks with iron frames and hinged seats. I was beside a girl who smelt of raw cabbage. The room was painted half brown, half green. It had a rough wooden floor that thundered to the sound of the teacher's heels. There was a blackboard on an easel and a fireplace in the corner, with a bucket of turf beside it and faded daisies in a jam-jar on the mantel-piece. There was a big picture of a guardian angel hovering over a small boy and his sister as they walked fearfully across a rickety bridge spanning a deep ravine. There was a smell of sour milk and dried urine.

Mrs O'Kelly went round the frightened throng of new prisoners and asked us all our names. She wrote them into the big roll-book. She could relate us all to members of our families who had preceded us. 'I hope you're not as thick as your brother was,' she said to some un-fortunate. 'I have enough stupid people here already,' she added, looking across at the High Babies, who cowered over their copies. We new recruits did not get copies, or paper, which seemed to be strictly rationed.

We were each given a small blackboard and a stub of chalk and were told to draw. Mrs O'Kelly walked among us with her arms folded, asking us in turn, 'What is that supposed to be?' and snorting in disdain at our shaky efforts to produce any likeness at all. It was as if she was preparing us for a lifetime of disapproval and failure.

When the school bell rang at eleven, we all went out to the yard for Small Play. The girls went out their own door to their yard and we went out another door to the boys' yard. There was an outside dry toilet – a green wall with a blocked gully and a cubicle with a hole in a wooden seat where your business plopped into a stinking cesspool below. Toilet paper was unheard of then: we used a bunch of grass or a dock leaf brought in from the yard if things were really bad. I hated the boys' yard – all the roughness of louts banging into you and knocking you over, calling names and fighting. Two boys were knocking spots off each other and a ring had formed around them, egging them on. There was a thin boy, who was pinned down by three rough tykes. One was sitting on his chest, another was straddling his feet, and the third was squeezing his testicles. He was screaming for all he was worth, but nobody seemed to care. I wanted to escape to the girls' yard, where I knew my sisters would take me by the hand and mind me, but all I could hear was their laughter from behind the wall.

I survived three years of Mrs O'Kelly, Low Babies, High Babies and First Class. I did learn. She sat beside me in the desk and showed me how to hold the pencil properly. There was one way and one way only, resting on the first knuckle of the middle finger, gripped firmly between index finger and thumb, slanted so that, if it were a gun, you could shoot a crow perched on your right shoulder. I kept looking at my shoulder to see whether the aim was right, and the pencil would stray and the back of Mrs O'Kelly's hand would land firmly on my jaw with a resounding smack. I would feel the ring on her finger like a knuckle-duster. In High Babies we graduated to Magnum Bonum pens, which we dipped in inkwells on the desk, and we copied headlines from the blackboard: 'May Day, delightful day.' 'The used key is always bright.'

We had to join all the letters: some had to go up to the top red line and some had to go down to the bottom red line and some had to stay within the blue lines. There was no room for mistakes or blots on the copy. We all wrote in unison, the teacher stalking the space between desks, flitting about like a bat, whining in her shrill voice, 'Up slant, down straight and rounded.' Then she would suddenly descend like a hawk on a boy whose pen had strayed and she would beat the living daylights out of him.

We learned a new Gaelic alphabet, with funny-shaped letters, some of which had dots on them called 'punks' and others that had slanted lines over them called *'síne fadas'*. We had to pronounce these Irish letters differently. 'A' was pronounced 'aw', the letter 'C' was pronounced like a 'K', and the letter 'G' was supposed to sound like the word 'gay'. It was all so confusing, learning two alphabets at once when you are only four, while at the same time keeping an eye out for blows on the head and crows perched on your shoulder.

We learned Irish rhymes, which were supposed to

train our ears to the sound of the language, but Mrs O'Kelly's Irish seemed different from the sounds of Irish that I was familiar with at home. My parents had Irish names for most things and my father could curse in Irish better that anyone. *'Buinneach gorm ort!'* he would say to someone who annoyed him, which means, 'May you have the blue diarrhoea.' The rhymes we learned in Low Babies seemed silly to us all:

> *Aon, dó, capall agus bó.*
> *Trí, ceathair, mála leathair.*
> *Cúig, sé, cupán tae.*
> *Seacht, ocht, sean-bhean bhocht.*

and
> *Lámh, lámh eile, a h-aon, a dó.*
> *Cos, cos eile, a h-aon a dó.*
> *Cluas, cluas eile, a h-aon a dó.*
> *Súil, súil eile, a h-aon a dó.*
> *Ceann, srón, béal, smig.*

We sang out the rhymes in unison, while the ogre at the top of the class conducted us with her switch. She would perch up on the desk like a buzzard, and her gimlet eyes would never leave us for a second.

When the Angelus bell boomed through the school from the nearby church, we had Catechism for half an hour. 'Now, children, pay attention,' Mrs O'Kelly would say. 'This half-hour may never come again.'

We prayed silently and fervently that it would, indeed, never come again – or any other half-hour in her malignant presence. She would settle herself in front of a big drawing of the Creation, with a bearded God stretching his hands out of the clouds and bringing mountains and seas and people into being. She seemed to have the story of Creation learned off by heart, because it was the same every day, word for word. Soon we knew it also, word for word. It always ended: 'He made the birds, the trees and the flowers. He wanted us to have a nice place to live in.' I remember wondering why He allowed Mrs O'Kelly in the world if He wanted us to have a nice place to live in.

I suppose I was lucky to survive those three formative years of Mrs O'Kelly without being too scarred. I was reasonably clever, and could escape the worst of her venomous cruelty. Others were not so lucky. Joe Murphy was slow and sleepy, and she laid into him with her fists and her switch almost every day. He was a big, tough lad, and he bore all the blows with hardly a murmur. It was as if he became immune to pain. He would never, ever cry, and this made Mrs O'Kelly all the madder. One day she cut his wrist with a stray blow of the rod, and he bled. The next morning his father was at the crossroads in Claran, just below the school. When Mrs O'Kelly arrived in her pony and trap, he made her go down on her knees in the middle of the road. Mrs O'Kelly spent the day sniffling and leaving the classroom and muttering something about 'a storm in a teacup'. Joe Murphy never appeared in Claran School again. He went to Clydagh School, where we must presume he was happier. When he left school, he became a builder in Galway and was in time a very wealthy man.

Stream of Memory

The stream that ran through our farm in the days of my childhood began in the marly *fáslachs* of Biggins's bog, where the snipe and the curlew and the teal-duck held sway. There were pike there too, in the plashy pools and silvery streamlets, but we never saw them – just a quick splash of a tail and a darting through the sedge and silvery grass, a shaking of the reeds and they were gone. We knew of older boys who hunted them with pitchforks, but my father said that a big pike could swallow a baby, so we never stepped barefooted into those glassy streams.

The water from this dark and desolate upland stretch of bog drained into a turlough beyond our mearing wall and then became our drain, our stream, and in our boyhood imaginations our singing river. It began tamely, snaking slowly through the Leana Mór, where the cowslips grew and where the cows drank on balmy summer days, swishing their tails to keep the horseflies at bay and standing belly-deep in the water to ward off the warble-fly. When they broke the banks and clogged the flowing water, my father would cut the soft sides steep again with the hay-knife, and we would pull out all the chickweed and rushes with a long-handled fork, which he had specially turned at the forge to make a drag.

Where the placid stream left the Leana Mór and flowed under the limestone wall by the plantation, it ran faster, downhill through Poll na Brafa, where it narrowed and twisted and bubbled over the rocks. There, at the little cish, we held our boat races. Our boats were tins with names like 'John West', 'Zam-Buk' and 'Sloan's Liniment', and they never made it far downstream without capsizing.

To that cish over the stream I came, with my mother, on a bleak November evening, to rinse out the pig's puddings. I remember the blue numbness of hands as the grime was swilled away and how she washed them, again and again, letting them flap away in the current like some white snakes that she tempted with a last taste of freedom before putting them, gleaming, into the enamel pail I carried. Those were the times when she must have had to fight her fragile nature, holding the bucket for the blood when the dreadful killing was done earlier that day on the heeled-up cart in the yard. Soon, however, in the steaming kitchen, she would scald and fill these white tubes with oatmeal and suet and onions and other magical aromatic things to make the best puddings in the village. We would be sent round the neighbours with a satchel full of puddings and liver and *gríscíns*. When you killed a pig, you shared, and so did they when their turn came.

Where the stream slowed down again to a round

curve under the hazel trees, there was a shady spot barely mottled with sunshine where the yellow primroses grew between the mossy rocks. Our sister, Mary, worked in the civil service in Dublin, but when she came home for the Easter holidays we led her by the hand to this secluded place to pick the fragrant flowers. We felt like native guides and in a way I suppose we were, leading a lost one back from a cold urban landscape to rekindle the fire of simplicity in her soul. By the time we had stuck the bunch of primroses in the *bunsop* of the thatch over our door, as the generations before us had done, the May Day ritual had reclaimed her.

The stream left our land through the high, shadowed arch under the road from Headford, where we would sneak, barefoot, into the cool, gleaming, wet-walled cavern and listen to the talk of grown-ups on the road above us. Voices drift down to me now, echoing in the cavern of my memory, voices of a people conditioned to ask questions but to give no answers.

'What kind of a fair had ye today, Joe?'

'Sheep and cattle.'

'How were cattle going?'

'Up and down the town.'

'What did you get for the calves?'

'Well, I didn't get what I was expecting. But I didn't expect what I got either.'

Receding footsteps then, and a white spit sailing down in a wide arc into the water, and my brother saying that I should have caught it in the sardine tin I was carrying. It was bound to have porter in it, and we all knew porter was poison. We could have killed a few pike in Biggins's bog.

My brothers soon grew old enough to help my father in the fields. I could still roam the banks and hide under the road, but it was never the same, somehow. My sister even sent me a blue-and-yellow plastic sailing boat in a parcel with red sealing wax on the knots, but the boat sailed too far and disappeared down the shore at the mearing wall, and though I ran frantically up and down along the whole length of the wall and waited at the other end until nightfall, I never saw it again. I lay awake in bed at night while the wind moaned in the thatch wondering where shores led to. Did they go right down to the centre of the earth? Was there a blue-and-yellow plastic boat sailing alone in some pitch-black cavern where light never shone? The best I could hope for was that this bright ship of my childhood would never sink like a sardine tin would.

The thought haunted my childish dreams until I came across a poem in my school reader called 'The Brook', by Alfred Lord Tennyson. The last verse killed off my nightmare forever. All streams lead to rivers and all rivers lead to the sea, and the sea spells freedom. And as long as the bright ship of your childhood can stay afloat in your dreams, you need have no fear:

> *And out again I curve and flow,*
> *To join the brimming river,*
> *For men may come and men may go,*
> *But I go on for ever.*

A Food for All Seasons

The world around us provided us with food for all seasons. We ate with the clock of the year, filling our bellies with whatever the day provided. When the hay-fork pulled up a bee's nest in the meadow, we covered it with a handful of hay until the bees had quietened down and then we came back and pulled out the honeycomb and ran for our lives. We gorged on the golden liquid that tasted of clover and sweet meadow-grass until our stomachs swelled with sweetness.

The *páirc bheag* was a land of brambles, hung heavy with blackberries, dark and juicy, with soft flesh like sweet wine on the tongue. We packed our stomachs till they cried out in swollen ecstasy. We filled shiny tin cans for our mother to make jam. We stole sugar from the dresser, brought it outside in our jacket pockets and made saucerfuls of our own concoction topped with dollops of cream from the dairy. We ate under the apple trees like gentry on the lawn.

In the first dewy mornings of July, when the sun spread its rosy light on the knee-high fog in the fields, we went forth in the startling coldness of the air to stir the cows from their beds in the grass and bring them in for milking. As we tried to bully them from their munching peace and drive their swaggering forms to the yard, we rubbed our sleep-encrusted eyes and watched out for the first mushrooms. When they appeared, overnight, like manna from heaven, we each raced to our own corner of a field, where there were a million last year and nobody knew, only to find that the vein of plenty had changed this year, and now there was a new bounteous slope somewhere else. We carried them home speared on a plantain stalk like a string of white pearls from a green sea.

There was only one way to cook mushrooms, and that was on the hearth. You broke off the stalk, put the rounded cup sitting on a red coal and sprinkled a pinch of salt in the middle. You sat and watched as the bubble of juice rose like a blister on the pink flesh, then you pounced and devoured, sucking in air and rolling the burning taste round on your tongue and sinking your teeth only once or twice maybe into a fleshiness that was raw and cooked and rare and burnt and tasted of the dew of the fields and turf-smoke and the salt of the giving earth. There had never been a taste like it and there never would be again.

For once on those heady mornings we had our own selfish agenda. We did not hunt together but alone. We rose from our beds even before our mother, who usually got up with the sun. Each of us had our own corner of the green world around us where we had staked a claim on the white-dotted manna from heaven. Each of us ate alone and guardedly beside the fire, hardly greeting another who would arrive alongside us at the hearth, pulling out coals from the raked fire in the greyness of the morning, with the blackbird barely clearing his throat outside and the world still sluggish in sleep.

The variety in our diet in those days was the variety that the year provided: when there was plenty of something, you ate it until it was gone, and then you waited for the tide of nature to turn and give you something new. What we ate was fresh; nothing was frozen or quick-dried or processed. There was no plastic or polythene. We never saw a tin of beans or a foil-wrapped anything, but we had turnips and cabbage and parsnips and carrots and lettuce and scallions all fresh from the teeming greenness around us.

July was a time of relative scarcity. The salted bacon was finished in the barrel, the old potatoes were getting wizened and waxen in the pit, and the new crops were not yet ripe in the fields. A little man called some Fridays selling herrings from a small blue Morris van. He was a brown, oily man with black eyes and he looked and smelled like a fish himself. We called him *'scadán'*, which is the Irish for 'herring'. He had a squeaky voice and he always said to my mother as he wrapped the fish in old newspaper: 'A Galway Bay herring roasting on the tongs – lovely, my dear!' Sometimes they were lovely, but sometimes we threw them out to the cat because they were so old that they smelt to high heaven.

And so as the dry, hazy days of July dragged on with no new taste on the tongue, my mother ventured warily for the first time to the ridge of new potatoes.

My father would always sow early potatoes in the garden near the house. They were meant for such a time as this, but my father cherished them like a child in the womb. He guarded them so that they would be left to complete their full gestation and not plucked untimely from the earth while they were still small as marbles. 'It's too soon yet,' he would say, after digging out an exploratory stalk. 'They're only *póiríns*.' But my mother would await her chance with the patience of a saint until he was away, maybe for a whole day cutting turf, and she knew he would come home tired and hungry and vulnerable. We would go out and dig up a bucketful or two of the yellow nuggets.

I can still see my aunt Molly, white-haired and smiling by the fire in the evening, scraping the copper skins from the new potatoes onto her lap, dipping the potatoes in the water, filling the big iron pot. And when they had boiled over the fire, my mother pounding them into pulp with a big iron fork that looked like Poseidon's trident, adding home-made butter and salt and a dash of milk. And then, timed to perfection, my father and my older brothers, sitting at the table with us, a castle of mashed *calley* on the plate in front of each one, a well in the centre of the mound for the melting knob of butter, scallions on the table to chop in. We ate silently, with spoons only. We swigged fresh milk and looked for second helpings. The world had turned its bountiful breast towards us again and the faint spectre of scarcity had vanished for another year. My father smiled and pushed back his chair and said a strange thing. 'The Lord have mercy on the dead,' he said.

In the brown days of early October, the dying year brought us a new bounty. As soon as the word was out, we emptied the books out of our satchels and headed to Carnacrow Wood to pick nuts. The hazel woods were full of colour, the leaves were golden and brown and russet and the sun shone into little clearings where some of the nuts had shelled and fallen on the matted ground. We picked the shiny shelled ones from the mossy ground and then we climbed into the branches for the nuts that still wore their half-tunic of green. If they shelled easily they were ripe; if their coats were obstinate they were unripe. We pulled them anyway, regardless of their readiness. This was one of the days of plenty; we might never be here again. The world might come to an end, or we might die, never knowing the sweetness of the sin of gluttony.

We sat on the rocks under the whispering hazel and broke the nuts open with stones. You had to be skilful: too hard a blow made everything mush, and you had to pick out splinters of shell. Some of the older boys could crack the nuts in their teeth and spit out the shells through the air with a 'thup' sound of the tongue. Some kernels were sweet as honey; some were raw as a cabbage stalk. It didn't matter. We ate them all regardless, old and new, sweet and sour. We filled our satchels and brought them home. We broke them open on the stone floor with the smoothing-iron. Walking across the kitchen then in your bare feet was a hazardous journey: you could find a sharp shell under your heel.

We always vowed to keep a store of nuts for another

Hallowe'en, but that seldom worked out. Greed held sway over husbandry and in that way we were like the first inhabitants of the earth. We ate sloes and fraughans and wild crab apples and elderberries whenever and wherever they appeared and there was many a hidden weevil that passed through our bodies unnoticed.

In many ways we were lucky. We were so close to the earth that we were immune to almost everything. Of course we got sick sometimes because of food, but it was nature's own sickness. When we gorged on blackberries we got diarrhoea. Excess of hazelnuts bound our bowels so tightly that it took them days to move. When we overdosed on mushrooms we raved like lunatics at night and our dreams were nightmare-ridden. But the balance in our bellies was the balance of the seasons, dictated by the turning earth. We never tasted preservative or artificial colouring or had to worry about a sell-by date. The fields were nurtured by farmyard manure, with a little help in the form of potash and sulphate of ammonia. Pests were controlled by proper crop rotation and not by pesticides. We were the only weedkillers my father needed. The only spray we ever saw was the magic mix of bluestone and washing soda to ward off the potato blight. Farmers in those days never made silage, and so the watercourses were pure and unpolluted and the wells held water that was as sweet and elemental as it was at the time of creation. Food was as simple as life and it was good to be young then and to taste on our tongues the true unembellished giving of the old land.

A-Hunting We Will Go

Where the hazel bank is steepest,
Where the shadow lies the deepest,
Where the clustering nuts fall free,
That's the way for Billy and me.

On Sunday afternoons, when farm work was stopped, and old men slept in chairs inside the window, and women chatted over china cups and the scattered crumbs of sponge-cake in the parlour, and girls walked the road showing off their dirndl skirts that came in a parcel from America, boys such as us hunted like Stone-Age savages for rabbits and foxes and badgers and hares and anything that moved on legs or swam in water. I don't remember us ever catching anything, but we were sure of our purpose. We were in our strong leather hobnails, armed with pointed scollops or bows and arrows we had fashioned from an ash-branch and a length of wax-end. On a lucky day we might have a fish-hook or a snare, or a gaff for the pike that lurked in the sedge. We were kings of the world, shouting our defiance at the wintry sun, running down slopes so that the wind filled our open mouths and took our breath away, and beating the brambles that blocked our way as if they were the English Roundheads that laid siege to Limerick and we were Sarsfield's men, fearless and bold and ready to face death.

We roamed and foraged in the wild upland bogs and the hazel woods and the furze-filled overgrown laneways that criss-crossed through the *páirc bheag,* a rambling, neglected tumble of scrubland that bordered our farm to the south, stretching all the way to the Carnacrow Wood. We followed those laneways, narrow and crooked as a ram's horn, lanes with old names like Boithrín Cam ('Crooked Lane') and Boithrín Cúng ('Narrow Lane'). These were built along the borders of old fields and farms, so they took up precious little space on either. Here and there they bulged into a passing-place for carts. Here and there too there was an old well, half-circled by a broken wall and some drooping mountain ash or beech, with water choked into a small black reflective pool by moss and water-cress, with a briar-leaf floating on it maybe, but when we stooped to drink from cupped hands that water was still as cool and clean as a sharp knife.

As a top-heavy toddler I struggled to keep up with my brothers as they plunged through unseen gaps in hedges where the stray strands of briar whipped at my face, or took death-defying jumps from the tops of stone *lochtas* that were as high as a schoolhouse, great big piles of limestone that had once been the walls of hovels and stables and carthouses and where, in the silence of an evening, we dreamed that we could hear people crying in the wind that whistled through the stones and the thorn trees. Hidden and buried in the long grey grass, we sometimes stumbled on the rusted iron head of a spade or a hay-fork that would crumble to the touch. Often, in the niches of the wall, we found the broken stem or bowl of a clay pipe, white as a bone, a chalky feel to it, reminding us of the wakes where they would be passed round. Even though at that time we were young and innocent, we had an awesome respect for those artefacts of the dead. We did not throw them away into the bushes. We tended to put them back. This place was like a sacred burial ground we did not want to disturb in case our steps were haunted by the unseen forms of a kind of holocaust.

Sometimes on those hunting expeditions I would baulk at the awful prospect of a jump over a bank of nettles, or the height of a wall in front of me, and my brothers would have to come back and lift me. Sometimes they got tired of me slowing their progress and made me run off home alone if we were not too far from the house.

I feared being left behind, for this was a wild and lonely place where long ago in an overpopulated land people had lived and struggled and died hungry, or left, pulling the door behind them, and leaving their tiny cabins to crumble into ivy-covered gables and lonely arch-stones standing now like gloomy sentinels in little clearings surrounded by briar-clumps and bushes grown thick and high as a church gable. There were myriads of little fields of every shape, now closed off and inaccessible, whose mossy surfaces still held the shape of potato-ridges, never dug out, made by men weak and waiting for the miracle of a crop that failed. We were told the stories by the fireside, and the ghosts of bony men and women, in *báiníns* and shawls, peopled our expeditions and stood before us at every turn of these tortuous laneways, plain as day in our vivid imaginations. Sometimes a barn owl or a pigeon would suddenly hoot his hollow note behind a high wall and we would freeze in mid-stride and look around us fearfully, half expecting a form to appear and challenge us on our journey.

There was one day when a form did appear – and frightened me so badly that I did not go hunting with my brothers for a long time afterwards. I had been left behind, alone on one of those winding laneways. The others had gone on when suddenly and without warning a black hag of a woman appeared round the twist of the lane. She was stooped and covered from head to toe in a black shawl. She carried a peeled *fás* in her hand that she used to sweep the nettles and stray brambles from in front of her stumbling steps. Her shawl was pulled so far out on her head that her face was barely visible but I could see two staring eyes as black as sloes, and high, bony cheekbones. Mortal fear rooted me to the spot where I stood by the wall of the lane, my screams petrified into silence at the back of my throat. She swept by me as if I was not there, her woolly shawl brushing my bare knees. She was moaning a low mantra that sounded like Irish. My brothers came back over the wall and saw her disappear around the next bend. 'It's Bridgie Ryder,' Pat said. 'That's her third trip today.'

I learned the story piecemeal. Bridgie Ryder was rambling, in her mind and body. *'Romháilte báis'*, my father called it: 'death's meanderings.' She was going back to her own people in the house where she was born, as a hare returns to its form. She had forgotten all her recent life, her married life in Knocklahard, where she had reared her family; all that part was wiped clean from the slate of her memory. She wanted to go home. She did this many times a day in these her last days. Her sons came and brought her back in the pony and trap, often twice and three times a day. They were very kind and good to her. They understood that this was the way of life. We all want to go home in the end. In those days people would not dream of sending someone to a nursing home. They would have deemed it a slur on their family. Old people were looked after at home by their families, eased into death by those they knew.

Soon I was back with the great Sunday hunting expeditions. I watched as my brothers set the snare by a break in a wall, where one stone on the grass would be a fatal jump for the rabbit. Pat, the oldest and wisest, showed us the marks of the run in the grass, where the rabbit always took the same bounding zigzag route. We rooted out the mouth of old shores which ran forever underground, and figured that there would be a badger in there sleeping, waiting for the sun to warm the earth around him.

We once had, for a precious time in those happy

hunting days, a fox terrier we called Ronnie. My father had brought it home to us one day in a shoebox, where the creature sat all quivering and tiny, looking up at us with sharp snout and baleful eyes that said 'Be my friend'. He grew up to be the height of the chair-rungs, playful as a kitten, and the light of our young lives. We took him hunting, and he followed every trail, but we had to lift him over walls. This day he went into the shore and disappeared. We could hear him barking and growling and we followed above ground and then we could hear a terrible battle where we believed he had cornered a badger or a fox. We could not dig through the rocks. We could only listen in agony. The night fell and the barking and growling died away and we went home crying and desperate. The following morning he was at the door of the house, all ragged and dishevelled and mucky, with a piece of his ear missing and one eye so badly scratched that it was no use to him again.

He never fully recovered from his ordeal, but he lived for another year to be our precious companion, and we planted in our minds a story of how he had killed a fox twice his size, the fox that had been stealing the hens for years, the terror of the neighbourhood. Ronnie eventually went blind, and kept bumping into things, and my father had to shoot him. We couldn't look or listen, we hid and covered our ears, but we buried him by the wall of the High Graffa, in the windy hill behind the house, and we marked the little mound of his grave with the empty cartridge case. I see the spot in my mind's eye, as it was then, under the cropped grass, a little bump in the ground of my past where a few tiny bones are covered. Like the undug potato ridges left behind by an older generation, we have left a mark, however small, on that old landscape. Unlike those frail men and women of the Famine times, we did not leave behind sickness and sorrow and death, but we buried there the fragile bones of innocence and the memory of tumbling days when we were all together under the wild sky.

I long to go back and find it, thinking, sometimes foolishly, that it would mean some sort of recovery. Maybe, when I'm like Bridgie Ryder, death's ramblings will compel me to hunt for home. But I know that the field is now as overgrown as the years are. It's better if I can remember it as it was.

Weeding Time

It's that time of year again when dandelions show their yellow heads above the grass and daisies are appearing on the lawn. I am told that it is time to operate.

For someone who was born and reared on a small farm in the era before pesticides, this is minor surgery, but it has a disturbing effect on me. I pull up my past with the roots. The smell of the wet clay brings me back to a beet field bounded by limestone walls. There are drills of sugar beet stretching ahead of me, green and glossy with recent rain, almost choked with weeds, and there are five of us – my older sister, my three brothers, my father and I – on our knees, crawling in the earth, thinning and weeding under a hot June sun. We have to leave one strong seedling at spaces of eight or nine inches, pull up the surplus plants and make sure that all the weeds are pulled as well.

My father's voice is carried back to me as I lag behind the others: 'Make sure you pull the roots. We don't want to see them growing again behind us.'

I do not want to be there. It's all right for the others, but I am only nine years old. I have a rag-nail that I am trying to bite. I can taste the salty earth. My knees are bound in hemp bags, tied above and below the knee with binder twine, but I can still feel the hardness of stones as I crawl painfully along. My father, up ahead, leans over to my drill and thins a bit for me so that I am now by his side. I can see his big, bony hands snaking under the crust of clay, digging deep to pull out root and clump. He shakes them like a terrier killing a rat, before firing them into the furrow where they will wither in the sun.

He knows each weed by its Gaelic name as passed down to him by his father and his father's father. *Ceathrú caorach, cupóg sráide, blisceán, fearbán, fliodh.* The *ceathrú caorach,* or sheepshank, is tall and easy to pull. He picks it up and flings it in the furrow as if it were a trump card that he was slapping on the kitchen table. The wily chickweed, or *fliodh*, requires a different approach. It creeps between the seedlings and fragments at the slightest touch. He plucks it between thumb and forefinger as if he were plucking the down from the breast of a goose. Whenever he comes to the hated dock, or *cupóg sraide,* he gouges into the earth with his calloused fingers to get the tapered end of the root. He grunts with satisfaction, calls it an ugly name, and continues his unyielding attack.

I never came to terms with weeding. I was defeated by it. The age-old, relentless and seemingly hopeless war against thistle and thorn was too much for me. I became a deserter. My aspirations went beyond the limestone walls and over the road to a place where I hoped weeds would never grow.

One by one we all left, and my father grew old in a changed landscape. Cattle grazed where there had been crops, and soon the sugar factory in Tuam closed its rusty gates for good.

But while he had life in him, he sharpened the scythe and went into the fields and cut the thistles, and if you watched his stooped frame stumbling towards the evening sun to bring in the cows, you would notice that he could never pass by a nettle growing near a fallen stone without swiping at it with his stick.

And as I crouch here now in the gloaming of my small suburban garden, letting the soil filter through my white hands, I get that old familiar feeling of something lost. In the shadow of the cherry tree I imagine, for a split second, that I see him, hunched over the soil, grappling with it, part of it, part of an ancient battle that was bounded by nature and nothing else, and I realise that in one short lifetime I have lost what it took centuries to celebrate.

Heart, Soul and Spirit

We were going to have the stations in our house, and that meant a party at night when all the fuss was over. I was sent with a note to Mike Ford's house in Carnacrow. He could play the melodeon. In fact, he was the only musician in the locality that you could call on at a moment's notice.

Mike Ford lived with his wife, Bridget. They had no family, but they seemed contented as the day was long. His house was small, his farm only a few acres overlooking the lake at Cargin. He was a wiry, wizened man, his fingers gnarled and bony, and his skin blue-black as the turf smoke. He smoked a crooked pipe, paring off the hard plug of walnut against his bent thumb, and when he looked up at me, his eyes were darting and restless as a swallow's flight. He was sitting in his favourite place on earth, beside the fire. You would not have much of a chance of seeing him on the road during the daytime, or even working in the fields, which were all in grass. He kept only dry cattle, and Bridget bought her butter and eggs from her neighbours.

Mike read the note I had brought, and then he stood

up and walked around the kitchen excitedly. 'Music is no good unless it's played with heart, soul and spirit,' he said. 'Heart, soul and spirit, that's what it's all about. Heart, soul and spirit.'

There was nobody else in the parish that had a musical instrument, except small Willie Carney, and he was too shy to play it outside his own house. But Mike Ford was available for station parties and homecomings and hooleys of all kinds. He would have been a godsend. The only problem was, he was as temperamental as Garvey's ass: sometimes he would start, and sometimes he would baulk.

Mike loved music too much. He knew three reels: 'Bonnie Kate' (in three parts), 'The Pigeon on the Gate' and 'Mrs McCloud's Reel', but halfway through one of them, he would remember how nice the other reel was as well, and he would stray into it for a while, and then he would try to find his way back, and get lost. He could play 'Shoe the Donkey' and a tune that you could dance 'The Stack of Barley' to, but not always at the right speed. And, of course, he could play a few old-time waltzes. But the whole night hinged on him. There was nothing else to dance to. All eyes and ears were on him.

Starting him up was the hardest part. Having coaxed him to take out the melodeon, relaxed him with a glass of whiskey, praised him to the skies and given him a chair beside the fire, everybody just waited with itchy feet for him to get a tune going. He started by drawing out the bellows to its full length and blasting the room out with a loud blare like a donkey's bray. Then a flutter of notes, a fixing of the strap over his shoulder, and a fragment of a tune and a pause. Then he wound himself up, feet tapping, knees hopping, shoulders going up and down like a threshing machine cranking into gear. His fingers flew over the keys like lightning and the music burst out in staccato spurts. Everybody held their breath and waited for a moment or two, hoping that he could keep the momentum going until the turn of the tune and beyond. Then they jumped onto the floor to show him that they loved to dance to his music, so that he could forget that he was the focus of attention, the key that unlocked the night of revelry. They shouted and whooped and swung and clattered the floor with their heels, and when the reel finished with a crashing crescendo they clapped and whistled their appreciation.

'Heart, soul and spirit. That's how music should be played,' Mike said, taking a sip from his glass of whiskey, hand and glass shaking with emotion.

'Heart, soul and spirit is right, Mike,' they all said, 'And it's you that can play it, surely.'

Then, without warning, he was off again headlong into another of his three reels, belting it out with gusto, and the crowd were on their feet again, swinging and whirling, knowing that this might not last the night. They had to make hay while the sun shone. The musician's whole frame hopped with the dancers, his forehead glistened with sweat, his elbow sharp against the glow of the fire behind him. He sucked and puffed his cheeks in time with the bellows, and his mouth made all sorts of contortions as his fingers found the clicking buttons on the accordion.

I sat in the chimney corner beside him, watching him in fascination. It was not the shiny accordion that fascinated me at all; it was the man's feet. They seemed to be crucial. They were like a vital cog in a machine. Every tune, every flutter of notes, started in the shoes. The heels lifted, the knees hopped, the shoulders joined in, then the elbow sawed and the head nodded and he was away, jerking the notes out of the bouncing box on his lap, forcing the dance and the tune to coalesce into one wild, precarious rhythm.

It must have been that wildness in the dance that brought out the devil in me, or maybe it was childish curiosity. On the pretext of stoking the fire, I slyly pushed a small *ciarán* of turf under Mike's right heel. It was as if the driving belt of the threshing machine had broken suddenly. In mid-dance, mid-tune, every-thing fractured and collapsed like a house of cards. The dancers stopped and looked at the musician in exasperation. Mike was not too sure what had hap-pened, but he was thrown totally out of kilter. He wiped his brow, swallowed all of his whiskey in one gulp and attempted to start again. The small fragment of turf was still there, blocking the starter-motor. He moved his chair, pulled another flurry of notes out of the melodeon and stopped again. He took down the shoulder strap and took out his pipe and tobacco. My father advanced with the whiskey bottle to top him up. My mother announced somewhat prematurely that there would be a cup of tea now.

Mike never really got started again that night, although there was a bit of a stop-start 'Stack o' Barley' and one or two old-time waltzes. Nobody ever knew what had made the music die. They blamed the whiskey. They spoke about the heat of the kitchen and the fact that Mike was not as young as he used to be. They never knew the truth.

In a few short years, the world had moved on. I was about sixteen years old when my father asked me to deliver a load of turf to Mike with the donkey and cart. Father Charlie had brought me a little plastic transistor radio from America. It was a wonder. I brought it with me everywhere in those days, my last, in the green valley. I mucked out the cow-byre to Elvis Presley's 'Jailhouse Rock'. I rattled down the boreen in the ass-cart to the strains of Chuck Berry.

After I had unloaded the turf, I went into the shadowy kitchen. I brought my wonderful transistor with me to show it to the man who loved music so much. It was a Saturday, and I thought we could catch the Walton's programme on Radio Éireann. He would like that surely. Mike was sitting at the fire, smoking his pipe as usual, and looking frail and old and sad now, bent over the faint red glow on the hearth. Bridget had died the previous year, and he never took down the melodeon now. Nobody asked him to.

The sun struggled to penetrate the small dusty panes of the window. The remnants of his dinner were on a plate beside him on the hob: the rind of a greasy rasher and the frazzled edges of a fried egg. I left the little transistor radio on the table and switched it on. Leo Maguire's programme was definitely over. The music that blared out was 'Rocking Goose' by Johnny and the Hurricanes. Mike looked as if he had been stabbed through the heart with a sharp knife. I fiddled ashamedly with the dials and got a tinny, crackling sound. I knew I could only get the one station anyway. I tried to make conversation with the old man but he only stared at the offending plastic box on the table as if it had just brought him the news that he was about to die.

I said goodbye and left him there by the fire. I hung the transistor radio on the crib of the cart and, when I was well away from the house, I switched it on again. Rick Nelson was singing 'Hello, Mary Lou, goodbye heart.' I looked back at the little house and thought how the small plastic box from America had fractured the last sad silence of that place.

'Goodbye heart' is right. Goodbye soul and spirit as well.

Sheep

Sheep were the white woolly galleons that sailed our sea of green when we were young. They dwarfed me when I first ventured, fearful and wary, beyond the garden gate. My first acquaintance was with a pet lamb that had been a companion beside the fire. He was orphaned at birth, brought in from the freezing January field and nourished with warm milk from a baby's sucking bottle. At first he nibbled at my bare toes but in no time at all he grew taller than myself, and stronger. He wanted to puck me with his head as if I were a shape that would yield milk to appease his insatiable appetite. He knocked me over easily and I had to be rescued, and he became another enemy that I had to run from.

You could say that my father was obsessive about the sheep. They had to be seen to, no matter what. They had to be counted every morning and every night before the sun went down. They were the first thing he enquired about if he had been away somewhere: 'Did anyone look at the sheep?'

The sheep that were reared on the farm in Carrowbeg were Galway sheep. They were a breed apart. They were pure white lowland sheep, not a trace of a black face among them, big and strong, and if you looked closely, each face was different. Their wool was thick and long, and white as the driven snow. I would say that my father's favourite part of farming, aside from plough-ing, was tending the sheep. He knew each one to look at. We would have them pinned in the corner and he would stalk around them and point out the ewes that had had twin lambs the previous year, or one that had slipped a lamb. He would sit a sheep down and dose it with some mysterious elixir from a small coloured bottle. I would hear the teeth grinding on the glass.

In the sultry days of August he walked through the fields watching for any one of them that might be making maggots. He knew the tell-tale signs: a sheep that would be turning back on itself, or trying to scratch itself against a tree or at a *puirín* in the wall. I would help him round them up into a corner of the field and he would pick out the one that needed to be relieved of the horrible itch that was driving it to distraction – the one that needed his care. He would find the nest in the fleece, cut away the wool, drench the spot with milky dip and shake away the demon dying pests, sending them flying everywhere, his teeth gritted in satisfaction, the sheep grunting as if in gratitude, man and beast in harmony, locked in an eternal, mutual dependence.

If he had noticed a sheep limping, he would open his sharp penknife and pare away the hoof until he found the trapped contamination, and he would scrape it out and bathe it in iodine or some potion that he had mixed in a bottle. He would never let a sheep go without dagging it, snipping away any dirty clots of wool. He was proud of the way they looked.

Sometimes we would find a sheep struggling, legs threshing, on her side, on the slope of a field, unable to get to her feet for a simple reason. A sheep will never roll downhill – no doubt remembering its origin in the dizzy mountain crags, fearing the crushing fall. There was such joy in releasing them, rolling them over, with the slope – against their instinct. They would leap away to freedom. But there were many stories of sheep that died neglected in such a state, unattended, uncared for, prisoners of their own fear.

The year had its own spaces for sheep. There was a time for washing and dipping and shearing and lambing. There was a small sheltered cove in the lake called *poll saileach,* or 'the sandy hole', where they were ducked and scrubbed and came out shaking and bleating in shock from the coldness of the grey-blue water. My father stood waist-deep in the water, and the men dragged the sheep one by one out to him and he would duck them underwater, getting their fleeces soaked, making sure their wool was clean. Then we would drive them home, trailing tracks of water dripping on the white, dusty road.

Shearing day was a day when the neighbours helped, a momentous day of flurry and fuss and we might have to stay home from school to help on a bright May day, herding the sheep into a corner of the front field beside the house, watching their thick fleeces shed from the nap of their skin, watching them walk away through the little iron gate into the next field shivering, looking embarrassed. We learned to tie the fleeces, stretching the white woolliness out on the green grass, turning in the edges like you would fold in the sleeves of a jumper, rolling them up with the outside in, tying them with the twisted neck-piece into a round soft bale that was carried to the barn.

In the barn on some dull wet day in October, when rain slanted in over the hawthorns in the High Graffa, my father would stitch and sew a multitude of hemp bags together into a huge woolpack, and the fleeces would be thrown down from the loft and packed into it and we would have to get in and trample and pack them tight and sometimes, in a space for childhood, we would fall on our backs in the flossy, clean-sprung whiteness and look up at the rafters of the barn and imagine we were on some magic woollen carpet floating away on the wind that whistled overhead.

When the time came, and my father thought the price was right, the bulging woolpack would be tied to the cart and brought to O'Grady's, where there would be haggling, often bitter and sharp. My father genuinely believed that his was the best, the cleanest wool. He could not understand why there was a fixed price, why everybody got the same per pound. That event usually ended with bitter recriminations. John O'Grady was crooked, someone would say. Didn't he make his money on the black market during the war, driving his lorry around Connemara selling tea and sugar and paraffin that were meant to have been rationed? He would never have luck. 'The crows will fly through his big sheds yet, you'll see if I'm right.'

Many years later, after all this old way had gone, and the sheep, too, had disappeared from Carrowbeg, as I saw from my car window the crumbling ruins of what had been O'Grady's empire, with the asbestos roofs half caved in, I recalled hearing a story from an old man shortly after my father's funeral.

I had driven down, alone, through the sad, wet, wintry midlands on a kind of futile pilgrimage of remembrance and regret. Dad was gone. He would never again appear at the grassy headland of a clay-filled field, leaning on the grey stones of the wall, his peaked cap set low under the fiery evening sun. His nailed boots would never again crunch the gravel round the empty yard that was once bountiful with lolling cows and sidestepping horses and the flurry and fret of work to be done on a bright, pristine-air-filled August morning.

And I, the one who never really thought I would, missed him. I missed him not just because he was my father, but also as the perpetrator and lord of all that was an old farm run with human sweat and trust in providence and little else. He had fought in the last bare-knuckle fight in Ireland between stubborn man and unrelenting soil. No tractor, no combine, no diesel fumes trailing, he tore and coaxed and wrestled that tiny valley of green into the full bounty of its giving. And when his upright, sinewy strength finally bowed and retreated into that silent house, there was nobody who would ever be willing again to fight such a fight. War on those terms was over. The old order was gone, and the weeds grew.

And if I tried to analyse why I headed west in that futile pilgrimage, I suppose it was because I wanted to convince myself that I was part of that lost struggle, that this car-driven, television-filled, mortgage-strangled life I now led had nothing to do with what I once had been. I arrived as evening fell. I sat in the silence of the kitchen. My mother would not talk; she had already resigned herself to the deliverance of her own death. I got into the car and drove to The Ferry, where he used to drink, endeavouring, out of a mood-driven desperation, to recreate some kind of comfort.

The place was deserted. No glow of light in the window, no boozy laugh or sweet smell of porter, just the rain dripping on the black windowsill and the sad, slow lapping of waves from the pier. I drove back there again the next day. The only customer inside was Patie MacDonagh, a distant cousin on my mother's side. He extended his sympathies on the loss of my father. I bought him a drink and we sat on the shiny wooden seat inside the front window that looked out on the grey-blue lake. You could see the gentle slopes of the Connemara Mountains behind the strip of water, mottled by the passing clouds.

'Sheep,' he said. 'Your father was a genius with sheep. Always got the best price for them too.'

He would make a long pause, but you knew it was a pause. The conversation was still taking shape, even through the studied silence. Pat Murphy brought over two more bottles of stout.

'He had a thing about sheep. It was no wonder, I suppose.'

Patie left a long pause between every few words he spoke. He held a smooth hazel walking stick between his knees. The silences were punctuated by the steady tapping of his stick on the floor, slow and regular like a metronome. It was as if he planned every few words and moved them about in his brain before he said them.

'His father had only one single sheep when he got the place. Used to drive it on its own back to Poll Sulach.'

Another long, tapping pause.

'His father before him had great trouble with the drink; nearly lost everything he had.'

The stick was quiet during the next intermission, but there was a tremor in the gnarled hand that held it. After staring at his drink for a long, wordless minute, he took the glass between finger and thumb and tilted it to his mouth, his elbow straight out and his little finger pointing up. There was a flourish about that last draining of the glass, as if he was toasting an unseen guest.

He looked at the empty glass, then put his hand on my shoulder and said, 'I must go. There's things to be done around the house.'

He took his cap from the seat beside him. 'There's a ghost that haunts us all,' he said.

BROWNE'S ISLAND

It was still dark when I was roused out of my warm bed. The air around me was still cold, though it was well into summer. My mother was fussing about the kitchen, wrapping things in scraps of newspaper and putting them into a satchel. There was a kind of mantra she kept repeating: 'Bread, butter and eggs. Tea, sugar and salt. Cups, spoons and knives.'

She would count them in the air with her finger, then rush off to get something that was missing.

My father was lacing his boots. 'You're coming to the bog with us today,' he said. 'There's footing to be done, as well as spreading. Hurry up and eat your breakfast.'

I had never been to the bog before. I was too young, and it was too far away.

I rode on the bar of my father's bicycle, hands on the handlebars, in the hollow of his hunched strength, his black jacket flapping like a tent around me. The *sleán,* a winged spade for cutting turf, was tied along the bar under me. The wind was sharp on my sleep-encrusted eyes, cold on my bare knees as we left the house, four bicycles in convoy on the dusty, winding road. We passed slumbering houses with barely a trickle of smoke from their chimneys. Sheep and cows still settled in their warm sets of grass, the dew around them like a glistening green sea. Only the thrush and blackbird were awake, their notes saluting us on our journey. We turned left at the top of the dead white town, down the Moyne road by the castle ruins and over the Black River into County Mayo. We did not meet a soul as our wheels whirred up and down the tiny drumlins where we were told the fairies lived, right after the haunted house at Shrule and then, when we reached Dangan, we veered right again and into the wide, unending landscape of bog-land that we called Browne's Island.

It could have been aptly called Brown Island, for it was just that: a dun, flat place stretching away into the distance on every side. Gone was the green-walled valley and the known blue ring of the Connemara Mountains. It was as if they had been swallowed up by a brown sea. White bog-cotton bobbed like flecks of foam on the waves of blown rushes. Piles of black turf dotted the landscape, some cone-shaped, some like the back of a great sleeping whale. Banks of greyish grass hunched over trapped pools of unmoving water that reflected the blue and white of the sky above. Here and there a bush or two, shaped by the prevailing wind, clung tenaciously to the sodden earth. No familiar bleat of lamb or low of calf here, only the lonely cry of the curlew and the eerie whisper of the wind through the sedge.

We left the ribbon of white road and turned in at a

little wooden *cish* to where our particular trench of turf lay, though how my father could identify it puzzled me. We left the bicycles under a bush and hung the two satchels on a branch, having submerged the bottle of milk in a pool to keep it fresh. My father went off and we stretched our legs on the spongy ground. When he came back there was a man with him who was the same colour as the bog-land around us. His name was Hubert, and he owned the stretch of bog we worked. He indicated the next bank of turf that we could cut. My father measured it out in feet, stepping carefully, heel to toe. He asked Hubert to step it out himself, but he laughingly refused, and you could see why: his feet were as big as boats. We would have got great value.

Soon we were set to work. Jim and I had to foot the turf that had been previously cut and spread on the bank. We had to stand the wet sods of turf on end, five standing against each other, with one across the top, so that the wind could whistle through them and blow them to a crusty dryness. It was back-breaking work. The sods were heavy and stuck to the wiry grass. Sometimes they would break in half, unless we lifted them like you would a sleeping child. The ground was uneven and the little sprigs of heather and furze made it hard to find a foundation for our tottering tents.

Meanwhile, my father had skinned the top of the next trench and already was waist-deep in the earth, slicing into the blackness dexterously with the winged *sleán* and pitching the wet sods up to the *eannach*, as we called the dry, uncut bank above. Pat and Michael fetched the sods in mid-air, softly cradling them so they would not break, stretching them out flat on the grass, where they would drain and get the sun. They were wet creatures, born out of the deep womb of the earth, sleeping until they had the strength to stand.

By midday my back was breaking and my limbs felt as if they were made of lead, but there was no let-up in the work. Any time I stood to straighten my back and gaze around me, my father would grunt something about how it was a waste of time bringing me to the bog if I couldn't work like the rest. I waited until his head was below ground level and eased off as much as I could. The bog around us had awoken to other black figures in the distance, wheeling barrows piled high with turf out of the wetness, building up drier turf into piles called *dúcháns*, shaped like big beehives. Some had taken the work a step further and had already put out their harvest into huge ricks by the road. They all seemed to work furiously, like ants. It was as if here, in this common place where all could be seen, there was a kind of race to see who was quickest and best. My father seemed to be caught up in that competitive urgency. He goaded and cajoled us and drove us, sometimes with a lightness of spirit, some-times with an explosive fury. His mood changed as often as the shade of that windswept place under the passing shadow of the clouds. Reluctantly, when the Angelus bell rang out faintly from some distant spire, he gave the signal for the meal.

Pat made a fire of scraps of brushwood and dried *ciaráns* of turf. He filled the kettle from one of the many clear springs, put the eggs in it and set it over the flame, replenishing it all the time. Soon we were wolfing down wedges of white soda bread and eggs, washed down with scalding tea. The tea was smoky and strong, but never again in my life would it taste so good, so vital to existence. There were even slices of brack to finish off. My mother, God bless her, had thought of everything. I lay back on the springy mattress of furze-roots beneath me and closed my eyes, imagining what she would be doing now in that far-off, now-alien world that I called home. A lark soared straight above me in full-throated song and the sun turned everything lemon-coloured behind my eyes.

I half-awoke to a coarse hand stroking my brow, a look of softness in my father's eyes near mine, a faint smell of tobacco. Then sleep overpowered me again. I dreamt of ships sailing on a blue sea between cliffs, pirates peering through spyglasses and treasure buried in a bog.

The sun was well into the western half of the sky when I awoke, dazed in the changed light. I then stumbled back to my post and struggled with the heavy wetness of sods again. Not a word was said about my lapse, not by my father nor, stranger still, by my brothers. There was clearly a pact, a resolution on their part not to taunt or chastise me.

When I rode again on the bar of my father's bike, I felt somehow more than shelter from the wind under the arch of his strength as we whizzed airily up and down over the fairy hills and all the way home.

The Last Stone in the Gable

There was definitely a noise downstairs. I raised my head off the pillow and listened again. I could hear a scraping, shuffling sound across the stone floor of the kitchen above which we slept. I elbowed the warm, snoring lump beside me in the little box-bed and whispered as loud as I dared: 'Jim! Wake up! There's someone downstairs!'

It took a minute for my older brother to respond. He rubbed his eyes and raised himself up on his elbows. We both listened. The silence was such that it had a ringing sound of its own.

'You're dreaming. Go back to sleep,' Jim replied.

'I know I heard something. Just wait a minute.'

There was a soft thud, followed by a faint, low moan.

'Maybe it's Mammy up early,' my brother said.

'But it's the middle of the night.'

The room over the kitchen, which was really only a large landing, was the darkest room in the house, and the faint greyness of the little window that overlooked the yard was the only shape visible now. Pitch darkness enveloped everything else all around. The room where our older brothers slept was on one side over our parents' bedroom and the girls slept in the other room over the parlour. Both doors were closed.

'I'm going to have a look,' Jim said, swinging his feet out of the bed. He was definitely braver than me, but then he was ten and I was only eight.

I remember following him stealthily down the six steps, avoiding the places that we knew would creak underfoot. We had to stand on our toes to peep through the gap over the stairs door. The red light of the Sacred Heart lamp cast an eerie glow round the big kitchen. With a start, we saw that there was a dark, human form stretched across the hearth in front of the fire.

'What will we do?' I whispered nervously.

'We'll wake Cecile.

Cecile woke up at the first soft call. She made us go back to bed while she went down quietly to investigate. When she came back up again she told us to go back to sleep. It was only Pat Carr, she said, who had come in off the road to warm himself. He would be gone in the morning. He was no harm to anyone.

Jim was soon a snoring lump in the bed beside me. But I could not sleep: I kept thinking about Pat Carr.

I learned a lot about him from listening to the grown-ups when they would be making hay or doing the threshing. Pat was a builder of walls, a stonemason of great skill and a mighty worker too, except that he drank so much. We often saw him staggering home from Headford, propped against his bicycle, barely able to stand. Once when I was at the road gate on my own, he stopped and mumbled something to me. I wanted to run in home, but I was mesmerised by his glassy stare, like a rabbit under the power of a weasel. He raised his speck-cap and fumbled in the pocket of his great frieze coat for a few Bull's Eyes that were stuck to a brown paper bag. My mother would not let me eat them. 'You wouldn't know what you'd get from them,' she said.

My father told us that Pat Carr was employed in the building of the new schoolhouse in 1936. They used some of the cut stone from Colonel Beddington's old manor house in Ower. When they were trying to knock the great high gable of the house, Pat hammered out a row of stones near the bottom of the wall, but the gable stood firm even when there was only one stone left in the middle of the row holding up the whole gable. It was a huge triangle balanced on one stone. All the workmen stood in fascination looking at it, wondering what to do next. Pat Carr suddenly rushed to the wall, struck the central stone a mighty blow of his sledgehammer and ran for safety as the whole gable tottered and swayed and came crashing down.

I remembered listening to the neighbours from across the road talking in the barn one day when they were winnowing oats with my father about how clever Pat Carr was and how, one night in Varley's, when someone was saying what a great invention electricity was, Pat corrected him quietly by saying that electricity was not an invention but a discovery. And I wondered, as the first faint upward gush of lemon-coloured light slowly brightened the little window of our room, how a man so brave and so clever should be stretched out on the hard hearth of someone else's house.

I heard my mother get up with the lark, as usual, to milk the cows. There was no scream of fright or indignation. It was not the first time someone had sheltered from the rain or cold. The door was never locked at night, and anyway, my mother was a quiet controller, a keeper of the peace.

I remember stealing down quietly once more to the stairs door, this time without waking my brother, and peeping down into the slowly brightening kitchen. My mother was bent over the prostrate form trying to wake him up.

'Get up, Pat. It's time to go home now.'

He gave a few grunts and made a feeble effort at movement.

'Get up. Come on now.'

The man struggled to prop himself on his elbow and then he faltered.

My mother tried to be firmer. 'Come on out of there,' she said, a touch of irritation coming into her voice as she tried to pull him into a standing position. 'Do you know where you are at all?'

Pat finally struggled to his feet and stood tall in front of my mother, drawing his two arms stiffly back and sticking out his chest as if he were bravely facing a firing squad.

Then I heard him speak in a loud, rasping voice. 'Well, I know I'm not in hell,' he said, 'for the fire would be a damn sight hotter than this.' He fixed his cap on his head and moved awkwardly towards the back door, my mother giving him a gentle push.

'And I'm sure I'm not in heaven either,' he said, 'for the Blessed Virgin would have a much kinder countenance than yours!'

I could hear the latch of the back door and then I heard my mother laugh quietly to herself as she made her way back towards the fire to hang the kettle on the crane. I stole up the stairs and into bed and felt a quiet kind of satisfaction surround me in the warm bed.

'What the bloody hell happened here?' My father's shout must have woken everybody in the house. Within minutes we were all in the kitchen in the bright morning light. It was soon clear what had happened. Pat Carr had burned my father's new shoes in the fire. This was Sunday morning, and the shoes had been left, polished, on the hearth to keep them warm. Poor Pat must have thought they were sods of turf and thrown them in the fire to keep out the chill. Now there were only a few charred pieces of leather and the remnants of one heel left in the smouldering ashes. I could see by my father's face that he was in a silent rage. Everybody hurried about trying not to get in his way, finding socks and shoes and queuing up for the basin in the scullery so we could wash our faces.

Getting ready for Mass was always a tense time anyway. Everything had to be right for my father. His collar had to be starched and his shoes polished, and there would be an unholy row if he couldn't find his collar stud, or his cuff links. He liked to hold his head up when he strode out to Mass in his Sunday best. But on this Sunday, he had to make do with his hobnail boots.

The next day, as we crept along the drills thinning turnips, we tried to immortalise the event in rhyme:

The night Pat Carr was on the booze,
He burned my father's Sunday shoes.

We made the rhyme out of earshot of my father, who was wary of ridicule. To be the butt of a joke swapped at fair or station house would be a fate worse than death.

It was a crisp Saturday in late December when my father and I were bringing ropes of hay to the cattle in the Heath Field. Johnny Frank pulled up on his bicycle with the news that Pat Carr's house had been burned to the ground the previous night.

'Sure 'twas a miracle that he escaped out of it at all. Only for someone was passing the house late after playing cards and saw the smoke, he would have been burned alive, and that's for sure.'

'What'll happen to him now?'

'Who knows?'

The two men were silent in their thoughts as Johnny kindled his pipe, cupping his hands to shield the match and sucking noisily before speaking again in his chirpy, high-pitched voice.

'Weren't you the lucky man that night when he came into yere house?'

I remember how my father looked up with a start into the other man's eyes, as if someone had landed a stinging blow to his cheek. This was the first time I had heard anyone dare to mention the incident in his hearing. There was an awkward silence. Then my father spoke.

'Well that's true for you,' he murmured, head down, as he pounded the ice in the roadside with the end of his stick.

When the other man had cycled away, my father hopped over the stile ahead of me, carrying the big rope of hay as if it were a feather. He whistled a fragment of a jig as he spread the hay out in little bundles for the snorting cattle to come and eat. Then he straightened his back and stood beside me. He laid a hand on my shoulder and surveyed the herd of cattle proudly. 'Will you look at the shine of them,' he said. 'They're as good as any bullocks this side of Headford.'

Pat Carr never got into a house at night again. If he could not make it to his own barn, he slept in the ditch. I don't know where he disappeared to, or what happened to him in the end, but I often lay awake in the little box-bed over the warm kitchen, listening to my father bolt the back door and thinking of the last brick being knocked out of the gable of the old manor house. In my mind's eye I could see all the beautiful cut stones come crashing down.

THE MIDDLE ROOM

I was much relieved to leave the Babies' room and go into Mrs O'Hanrahan's. She taught second, third and fourth classes. Maybe 'taught' is the wrong word. She listened to us learning, and pointed out a few things that we might be getting wrong along the way. She was a woman of ample proportions and she seldom left her chair except to stand in front of the fire and pull up her skirt at the back so she could roast her behind. She would ask, 'Do you feel the heat, children?' but of course we did not, because she blocked the whole fireplace with her body.

Her first priority every morning was to have two boys from the master's room come in to kindle the fire. The turf from the shed was usually damp and the chimney was poor, so the room would quickly fill up with smoke. She would not start until there was a blaze, which took half the morning. Then she set to question everybody, not about their schoolwork, but about news from home, for she was the most curious gossipmonger I ever met in my whole life. The girls loved to pander to her curiosity; the rest of us just filled in the time,

Despite Mrs O'Hanrahan's lack of dynamic teaching skills, I progressed in my learning from Second Class through Fourth. In Second Class we got our first school books: a short Catechism, an Irish book, a model arithmetic and, best of all, an English book whose pages smelled of newness and which had pictures and poems that sent my imagination soaring beyond that dull room and the teacher who never left her chair. It was the poems in those little books that somehow struck a special chord with me. I learned them easily; their rhyme and rhythm flowed round my ready mind like liquid honey in a jar. Verses lodged in that uncluttered brain and for some strange reason come back to me still:

Welcome, red and roundy sun,
Dropping lowly in the west;
Now my hard day's work is done,
I'm as happy as the best.

I can still see the beautifully simple line drawing of the woodcutter walking home through the trees to the big red ball of the setting sun on the horizon. Many of the poems had a religious theme, a lesson to impart about the value of humility or the dignity of labour. I can see a picture of Our Lady sweeping the floor, a wooden cradle beside her:

The large and lovely lessons
You taught with little breath
In the liturgy of labour
In the house of Nazareth

Are such fantastic simple things
That mortals may presume
To call the Queen of Seraphim
Our Lady of the Broom.

Half of the words I did not understand, and 'Mrs O.', as we called her, did not bother herself too much about explaining them, but I fell in love with the sound of them, the way they tripped off the tongue and made me feel important somehow. And I fell for the way these magical poems could carry you on their wings to places and feelings that were new and sad and happy at the same time:

The coach is at the door at last;
The eager children, mounting fast
And kissing hands in chorus, sing,
'Goodbye, goodbye, to everything!'

Then there was a little poem that has reverberated in my mind ever since: a picture of a cottage under the mountains, beside a lake with water lilies and sedges. I remember it in its entirety, and whenever I dream about that far-off time when I was a boy growing up in the hollow of nature's hand, whenever memories of home haunt me, these simple lines are never far away:

Blow high, blow low,
O wind from the west,
You come from the country
I love the best.

O say have the lilies
Yet lifted their heads
Above the lake-water
That ripples and spreads?

Do the little sedges
Still shake with delight,
And whisper together
All through the night?

Have the mountains the purple
I used to love,
And peace about them,
Around and above?

O wind from the west,
Blow high, blow low,
You come from the country
I loved long ago.

Of course I learned other things, like sums and tables and spelling. Mrs O. gave us endless rounds of dictation, which she had us correct ourselves by having us swap our copies and count our mistakes. We formed a ring around her desk by the fire, and she examined our tables one by one. We stumbled through tables with money, prompting each other, coughing when we were stuck, distracting the teacher whenever we could. Sometimes we droned out the tables in unison in a flat, monotonous dirge:

Two sevens are fourteen pence, one and two-
pence;
Three sevens are twenty-one pence, one and nine-
pence;
Four sevens are twenty-eight pence, two and four-
pence;
Five sevens are thirty-five pence, two and eleven-
pence.

We learned our Catechism every day when the Angelus rang, the Commandments of God and the Command-ments of the Church, the eight beatitudes and the seven deadly sins, the gifts of the Holy Ghost and the four cardinal virtues. We had to have our answers word-perfect, for our whole religion was based on knowledge of its definitions. We learned the difference between sanctifying grace and actual grace, that those who die in mortal sin go to hell for all eternity, that purgatory 'is a place or state of punishment where some souls suffer for a time before they can enter heaven'. We learned that, according to the Fourth Commandment, we honour our parents 'by treating them always with respect, by showing gratitude to them, and by bearing patiently with their faults and weaknesses.' We had to memorize the fact that the Sixth Commandment forbade not only adultery but also 'all immodest actions, looks or words, and everything that is contrary to chastity' and that the Eighth forbade us 'to tell lies, to injure our neighbour's character or to make known his secrets.'

Once every year there was a flurry of excitement

and anxiety when the diocesan examiners came – two sharp men of the cloth from the bishop's house, ready to trap us if we slipped up in our knowledge of the Catechism. The parish priest worried about the prospect of the unspeakable indignity of his school getting a low mark. The master worried, even Mrs O. fretted, sometimes, unbelievably, leaving her seat by the fire to pound the Catechism into us. We learned the Catechism every day, all day long for weeks before the dreaded day. Bright pupils were encouraged to answer. Those who were slow were told not to put up their hands.

I remember the last diocesan examination in that middle room, Martin Maille standing, red-faced and struggling, fixed in the beady eye of the examiner. Martin was slow to speak, quiet as the woods in Ballinacregg where he grew up, thinking deeply about his answer. 'How should we pray?' the priest had asked, clicking his fingers impatiently, eyes flitting over the bowed heads of the boys in the class until he alighted on Martin. Martin looked up eventually at the priest and said, 'We should be kneeling down.' The priest glared and pointed to Veronica Toole, who was sawing the air with her hand. She sang out the answer: 'We should pray with a humble and contrite heart, with attention and perseverance, with confidence in God's goodness and resignation to his will, and in the name of Jesus Christ.' The priest was satisfied. Mrs O. breathed a sigh of relief.

BILLY AND HIS SEVEN BARRELS

'In the name of all that's holy, will you come away from the window! Your eyes will go crooked watching that hill.'

My mother was right, as usual. I was perched at the front window of the kitchen, where the thick stone walls afforded ample sitting room for a small boy, and my face was so close to the pane that my breath was clouding the glass and my vision had begun to blur. I could still see the top of Carrowbeg Hill, where a lone bush jutted into the grey December sky. That's the spot where we always hoped to catch the first glimpse of any visitor, and that's where the visitor would catch the first view of our tidy, ivy-covered thatched farmhouse, nestling between the corn-stacks of the haggard and the copper-beech tree that my grandad had set.

I came away from the window and sat in the hob, under the arch of the fireplace. It was Christmas Eve and my mother had no time for idle youngsters. All morning she had fussed and fretted round the house, while I pretended to help and tried not to get in her way. There was not much a nine-year-old boy could do, anyway, that she would accept as satisfactory. 'I'm the best to do that,' she would say, not in any boastful way but as a mere statement of fact, a quiet assertion of self-belief.

The kitchen was, indeed, a credit to her industry. Before anyone else had risen from their beds that morning, she had been busy with the whitewash-brush, whitening the chimney behind the fire, leaving only a straight, dark, even road in the middle for the smoke to travel upwards to the broad chimney. When I came down the creaking stairs that morning, she was on her knees in the cold half-light at the fireside, scrubbing the hearth clean. As the first light of day stole in through the small back window, I watched, chin in hand, as she scoured the crane and pothooks with the wire pot-scrub and blackened the iron cover that sealed off the ash-pit under the hob. My gaze followed as she walked in from the scullery with the great big kettle to hang over the fire for the morning tea.

Even then, at fifty years of age, she was stooped and toil-worn. Her fingers were calloused and her eyesight was beginning to fail, a result of too much sewing and darning under a poor oil lamp. We had only got the electricity a year earlier and she still scrubbed the clothes on the washboard and baked in the oven over the open fire. The ceaseless cackle of my grandmother, the unceasing demands of children, the constant struggle to rear a family on twenty-five acres – all had taken their toll. But she had an unshakeable belief that all would be well in the end, that 'God does all things for the best', as she would say. She took one thing at a time. Right now she was just glad that her eldest daughter, Mary, was coming home from Dublin for Christmas.

'What time will she be coming?' I kept asking the same question all morning. By now it was four o'clock and my mother was pulling the last pin-feathers out of the big goose on the kitchen table.

'For the umpteenth time, I don't know,' she answered irritably. 'Go out and help your father and stop annoying me.'

It was better outside. Time seemed to pass quicker in the freedom of the cold, frosty air. My father was at the pit of potatoes, stripping off the covering of stalks and scraping down the coat of clay as far as the straw, to reveal finally the neat conical pile of potatoes, all snug from the winter frost. He had two buckets, one on each side of him. 'Put the little poreens in that one,' he said. 'We'll keep them for the pigs. We need nice fat floury ones for Christmas Day. Don't forget the lovely potato stuffing Mammy has to put in the goose!' When we had brought the potatoes in, I helped him sweep the yard and then we fixed a nice tight sheaf of straw outside the back door. He trimmed off both ends with the big hay-knife.

'Now, people won't be bringing muck into Mammy's nice kitchen, and the place will be grand and clean when Mary comes,' he said.

'What time is she coming?' Again the same question.

'It depends on whether she gets a lift from the station. If she doesn't, she could be very late, and you'll be in bed,' he said, looking meaningfully from under the peak of his cap.

'She could get a lift in Flaherty's van,' I suggested, quickly cheering myself up. 'She should, with the help of God,' he answered. 'Now come on and we'll get the holly.'

My heart rose. The Flahertys would surely give her a lift, and she would be home much sooner than if she had to wait for the Ballina bus. The Flahertys owned the local shop and went to Galway almost every weekend to sell the eggs and potatoes and cabbage that they took from the local farmers in part exchange for the tea, sugar, paraffin oil and other commodities that they sold. Mrs Flaherty was a nice woman, and she liked me because I served Mass. I knew she would give Mary a lift. The night before, when my mother was polishing the eggs with bread soda, I had slipped a note into the basket. 'Please, Mam, give Mary a lift home on Christmas Eve.' It was written on a piece of tea-paper, which was all I could find, and the pencil was not pared very well, but I felt sure that she would find it.

Mary was now in the civil service in Dublin and for the past four Christmases she had come home on the train on Christmas Eve. She always brought a present for everyone in the house. And they were good presents – better than what Santa Claus could manage. Each year seemed to surpass the one before. Last year had been the best of all. She'd brought me 'Billy and His Seven Barrels'. It was a wooden barrel the size of an orange, and when you opened it, in the middle there was another barrel, and so on until you found Billy, a tiny wooden boy with a painted smile, inside the last, tiny barrel. I really loved that toy. Through all the lengthening days of spring I had played with it everywhere, out in the haggard and up in the loft of the barn when the rain drummed on the corrugated metal roof. When the wind whistled in the thatch, I kept Billy snug beside me in my bed under the eaves, and whenever I felt sad all I had to do was release the little smiling boy. All the trouble of opening the barrels was worthwhile in the end when you could take him out and make him run through the folds of the pillow or outside in the grass of the lawn, which must have been like a jungle for him.

Then, on threshing day, when I took him out to show him the great orange-coloured machine with the menacing moving belt from the Fordson tractor and the straw flying away from the monster's mouth, I lost him, and he got covered up in the tumult of straw and chaff.

I remember searching for hours but I knew that I would never find the smiling boy again. I replaced him with a glass marble inside the seventh barrel, but it was never the same somehow. There was no way I could pretend that the marble smiled.

'What will she bring me this year, I wonder?' This was the question that went round and round in my head as my father cut the holly branches and we carried them home in the early misty darkness. It stayed with me as I handed the sprigs of holly to my mother to place behind every picture in the bright, white-walled kitchen that smelled of suet and spice and jelly and Christmas treats. 'What will she bring me this year?' I wondered, as I held the chair for my mother at the big wardrobe upstairs where she went to take down the box with the decorations and the little cut-out Crib. 'I wish for something like last year,' I prayed silently behind closed eyes as I placed the penny candle in the shoe-polish lid in front of the crib.

Then, suddenly, there she was, landed in the middle of the kitchen floor, with her big suitcase and her bags and her scent of perfume and air of city shops and mysterious wonder. 'Oh Lord,' said my mother, 'and not even a chance to change my apron!' 'Oh, the house looks lovely, Mother,' Mary said. 'I never saw it looking so nice.' There seemed to be an eternity of talk before the suitcase was opened. Then there was the frantic breaking of string and tearing of paper. A box. A Lone Ranger pair of six-guns and two holsters! It was as good a present as I could have hoped for.

Later, when we all sat down to the 'Big Supper', as we always called that special meal on Christmas Eve, with the Christmas candle burning brightly in the front window seat where I had perched all morning, and with my guns strapped tightly to my thighs, I listened to the grown-up talk.

'So you are serious about this fellow, then?' my mother asked, probing.

'He's a very nice lad, Mother. He comes from Roscommon – a big family, just like ours. And he has a good job in Guinness's Brewery. But he doesn't drink, mind you!' Mary said, turning to my father.

'Oh, leave him where he is, so!' laughed my father as he lit up his new briar pipe.

'I know you don't mean a word of it, Daddy. As a matter of fact, we are thinking of tying the knot in June.'

There was a general air of celebration and congratulations and my father had his pre-Christmas glass of whiskey, but when the dishes were all cleared away and the Rosary was said, Mary found me crying behind the churn in the darkened corner of the scullery. 'What's wrong?' she coaxed, putting her arm around my shoulder.

'I lost Billy, the smiling boy,' I lied, as best I could. Even in the half-darkness I could see that her eyes, too, shone with tears. We both knew that Christmas would never be the same again.

THE TURKEY THROTTLE

It may seem strange, but talk of turkeys does not remind me of Christmas at all. I see myself cycling down a white dusty country road, past limestone walls and under the dappled canopy of trees in the heat of a bright spring day. My friend and neighbour, Joe Biggins, his tousled head thrown back, is cycling beside me, confidently bobbing up and down on the pedals of his mother's High Nelly. We were both about nine years old, but we were entrusted with a very serious mission.

Hanging from the handlebars of my bike was a satchel, and in that satchel was my mother's pride and joy: a big fat hen turkey that would, if all went according to plan, produce a nice clutch of chicks that she could fatten for Christmas. The turkey's neck stuck up proudly from a small opening in the top of the bag. Joe's Mammy had given her turkey a pillion passenger's seat in a cardboard box on Joe's carrier, the box all bound with binder-twine. Her turkey's neck, too, was like a periscope in the air. There was a smell of hawthorn in the hedges as we passed two men sowing turnips in a field by the road. They looked up and scratched their heads. Two small boys on bicycles, carrying two turkeys.

We were heading for Nohilly's in Cordarra. They had a prize turkey cock. Now you probably get the picture. Our mammy turkeys were going on a kind of honeymoon, a little bit of fun in the sun. You could even sense that they were full of a kind of frenetic anticipation. They gobbled incessantly to each other and fidgeted restlessly within the confines of their respective accommodations. Joe said he wished he understood turkey-language. Even though we were only nine years old, we felt somehow that we were playing some important part in the great process of nature.

But no great mission is without its element of danger. Because I was so small, I had to ride my father's bike with my right foot under the crossbar, so that the bike tilted at a crazy angle to the road. It soon became clear to me that Biggins's turkey was travelling first-class. Mine was down with the steerage. As we whizzed down the hill past the graveyard, the satchel was swaying precariously and bumping against the wheel of the bicycle.

Then the unthinkable happened. As I swerved to avoid a pothole, the turkey managed to stick its head between the spokes. There was a sudden strumming sound as if from a dull harp and the bicycle came to a halt.

Death must have been instantaneous. There was no blood, but the turkey's neck, when I managed to extricate it, was considerably longer than it had been. The bird looked more like a kind of a hairy swan. There was a mystified look in its eye.

Joe Biggins insisted that we continue on to the end of the road. 'We might as well get half the job done, anyway,' he said.

We watched from outside a small corral as his protégée did the turkey trot with her newfound mate. She seemed to be a reluctant lover. I knew that her heart wasn't really in it because she kept running away. I figured that she missed her companion, but Joe said 'They're always like that.' He was very wise for a nine-year-old.

When I finally got home, my mother was very upset. 'There goes the few extra pounds I was counting on at Christmas,' she said. My father took one look at the distorted corpse lying in the yard and burst into an uncontrollable fit of laughter. 'It's a pity it didn't happen on the way home,' he said. 'She would at least have died a happy death.' He put his arm around my mother there, in the middle of the yard! I could see that she was laughing too. I just walked away.

I was in no mood then to witness another turkey trot, but every Christmas, when I see the basted bird on the table, I smile to myself and wonder if she died happy.

I Hear Lake Waters Lapping

The green valley where I grew up was about a mile and a half from Lough Corrib, at the nearest point in Annakeen. The lake circled our world to the west. When we worked in the high fields, we could see its thin blue line all around us, stretching from Cong in the north to Annaghdown in the south, with the Connemara Mountains all mottled in muted colours behind it. The lake was a presence in our lives. It loomed large in our days, past and present. It was a giant, a well of old stories, a deep threatening monster, a heaving swell of history and a placid place with sandy coves where you could bathe in the sultry August evenings. Its dark waves moaned of drownings and partings and monster pike. It had been a barrier long ago against the 'Ferocious O'Flahertys', who marauded and plundered from the wilds of Connemara. Its shores were dotted with the ruins of Norman keeps, at Clydagh and Annakeen and Ballycurrin.

In our childhood Sunday wanderings, we crept into the keeps' silent interiors and lived again the history of conquest, seeing the ledge from which prisoners

into the blackness of the deep water. It seemed like an eternity before the bottom of the boat scraped on the gravel of the island. I was lifted out onto the heaven that was solid land under my rubbery legs.

The island was almost entirely covered in trees, all tangled and leaning eastwards with the prevailing wind. In a clearing beside the broken pier were the remains of a wooden house, with green and white paint peeling from the boards. It was like an old tumbledown cricket pavilion with a verandah to the front. Its windows were broken, the door was missing and the roof was caving in. We went inside into the gloom. There were some tables and chairs and a rusting iron bed, but what I remember most of all were the old books that were scattered everywhere, with damp pages and musty covers turning green. There were Bibles and prayer books and books about gardening and fly-fishing. There were lined copybooks, the pages mostly stuck together, filled with pressed flowers, their names handwritten in faded ink. The place was filled now with the song of finches and blackbirds from the woods and the sweet smell of the honeysuckle that grew in profusion round the windows.

Later I learned of the man who came to live there, in that wild and lonely spot: a Protestant clergyman from England, with his gentle wife. They built that wooden house and lived in the quiet shelter of the trees, surrounded by the lapping lake water. They never left the island; a local man brought them provisions from the village – salt and sugar and flour and paraffin for their lamp. The turf-boat called twice a year. They grew potatoes and vegetables in a little plot beside the house. They fished for brown trout and salmon in the lake. They kept entirely to themselves.

When the clergyman died, his wife buried his body in the garden, but she kept his spirit alive so that loneliness would not devour her. She laid out his pipe and slippers every night and talked to his ghost beside the wood-stove. She prepared meals for him at the table and asked him if he liked the grilled trout, and she warned him to be careful of the bones. And his spirit answered her, forming the words from within herself, and so she herself was able for a while to hang on to the life she had on that quiet island far from the place from which she came.

We broke the swimming rule as well, on a sultry evening one August, after a day spent making a sheep-cock. The air was heavy and humid, with dark thunder-clouds threatening. The midges swarmed round our sweaty skin and nipped incessantly. Our eyelids were thick with hay-dust, our clothes were clammy, and our arms and necks were burnt raw with the sun and crying out for the coolness of the water that we knew was only a mile away. We stole away, four of us on two bicycles, back the road and up the bumpy boreen at Annaghkeen and through the brambly cow-patted field to *poll saileach*, the sandy-bottomed cove hidden from the world. We threw our clothes on the furze bushes and waded waist-deep, shoulder-deep into the still water, our feet on the sand and our hearts in heaven. We splashed and plunged and dunked our dust-filled heads and made thrashing, futile attempts at swim-ming. We banged our toes and knees on the sharp rocks around us but we didn't care.

While we frolicked, the evening suddenly darkened and the sun died. The air grew even more humid. For once the mistle thrush and the blackbird were silent. Swallows knifed so low through the air their wings tipped the water. A faint wind rose for a moment and then it was deadly calm again, but the leaden clouds were locked above us. A single drop of rain on the surface of the water and a clap of thunder like a load of turnips tumbling from a cart and we were out and pulling clothes on our wet skin and running madly for our bikes. The lightning flashed and we counted the seconds to the thunderclap as my brothers pedalled for all they were worth. We were racing for our lives. I had to jump off the bar and run up the hills with the bike and then hop on again. It was the worst thunderstorm we had ever seen, the forked lightning cascading like lava down the edge of the clouds, the sharp crack of the thunder like a rifle now, and immediately the swish of the lightning bolt on the grass beside us, not even a second separating peal and flash. We could smell the sulphur in the air and we promised God that we would all be priests and spend our lives in Africa if only he saved us now.

We were sent straight to bed, but though we hid under the bedclothes the lightning burned on our vision like the fires of hell, and each thunderclap was the booming voice of God saying, 'Swimming is forbidden. Fourth, honour thy father and thy mother.' When fitful sleep finally overpowered us, our dreams were of the Fall of Adam and the Plagues of Egypt, and the words 'Depart from me ye wicked' were emblazoned in lightning across the dark sky.

THE MAYFLY BOX

It was hay-time. The smell of the new-mown grass seemed to penetrate everywhere, even into the kitchen, where my father was working himself into a frenzy trying to get us out of our beds and into the hay-field now that the unexpected good weather had necessitated an early cut.

'Half the country is gone to and fro and you're all still in your beds!' he shouted up the stairs to the room where the three of us were trying to get the shrams out of our eyes. 'Get up quick or I'll go up and pull ye out!'

Michael and Jim, who were twins, and two years older than me, were already half dressed. I felt the cold linoleum on the soles of my feet and groaned. I hated the hay. The hay-dust blocked my nose and the musty smell made me sick. It was all right for my brothers: they were allowed rake and make hay-ropes and they didn't get the frightening job of tramping the haycock.

I pulled on my short trousers, stuffed in the tail of my shirt and shuffled sleepily over to the small window where I had kept the shoebox overnight. My heart sank when I noticed that someone had removed the clothes-brush that I had used to keep the sash open. I was almost afraid to look inside. They were still alive, but only just. I pulled on my socks and struggled into my unopened shoes, tucked the box under my arm and stole down the stairs. Avoiding the creaky step, I was able to peer into the kitchen through the crack in the stairs door. I could hear my mother in the scullery, straining the milk. My father must be out at the hay already. A minute later, I was rattling down the bumpy lane on my mother's bicycle, standing on the pedals. My only worry was the box on the carrier and the precious cargo inside. I only hoped that the wind that blew up from the lake would revive them. There was a blackness on their wings this morning that I knew was unhealthy.

Hubert Creaven was putting the landing net into the larch boat as I came down the lane to his house. He stood and watched me steering my way around the bumps and potholes. I parked the bicycle against the fuchsia hedge and bounded over to him, with the white shoebox held towards him as if it were an offering made to the gods.

'I got eighteen last night, Mister Creaven, and I couldn't bring them over 'cos I had to slice the turnips and feed the calves and then it was too late, but I kept them near the window and left it open, only someone closed it durin' the night and I hope they're all right,' I panted, 'Mister Creaven,' I finished, when I had finally caught my breath. Hubert Creaven seemed to be watching the curls on the top of my round head dance in the sudden light wind that blew up from the lake. A hint of sadness appeared to pass briefly over his kind, wrinkled face as the shadow of a cloud might pass over the water. He took the box in his gnarled hand and lifted the lid gingerly.

'Oh dear, dear!' he murmured in the soft, mellow voice that was such a contrast to the bustling urgency of my father's.

'I'm afraid things don't look too good.'

I was devastated. 'But I picked them out of the bushes yesterday, Mister Creaven. They looked so green and fresh. They were the same colour as the hawthorn leaves.'

Hubert Creaven moved aside on the seat of the boat and stretched out his hand to help me in so that we could both sit together. I could smell the turf-smoke from his jacket and a strange, sweet smell from his breath.

'I can't stay long, Mister Creaven. They're making hay at home and I have to be back before they have the first meadow-cock made or my father will kill me.'

The old man looked thoughtfully into the box and smiled his wistful smile. 'The mayfly hasn't long to stay either, Tommy,' he murmured, without shifting his gaze from the box. 'We'll let these ones die in the open, where they belong.'

With that he tipped the box and let the wind carry the fragile flies away towards the hedge. Some of them struggled to get out, and I watched the slow, deliberate movements of the man as he picked them out one by one by their fragile wings and held them up until the wind from the lake carried them away and they were lost in the tangle of grass and sedge by the shore.

My mind was in turmoil. I saw one and sixpence blown away on the wind, but somehow I felt glad for the mayflies that had escaped the jaws of the trout. It was an awful death, even worse than my own death that I had imagined last night, toppling over from the top of a high meadow-cock onto the hay-fork that my father was holding up. The worst thing was, I would not get to the matinée in the town hall on Sunday. I had seen the poster in Varley's window: *Shoot-out at Medicine Bend,* starring Randolph Scott. It was bound to be a cracker. Then I felt Hubert's hand on my shoulder.

'Come with me, I won't keep you a minute,' he said over his shoulder as he led the way towards the house.

Hubert's wife was there in the doorway – a bright, pleasant, round-faced woman in a crossover apron.

'Well, fancy that now,' she said as she rubbed her plump fingers together. She was always very good to me. She would give me a freshly baked scone and a glass of raspberry cordial, all set out neatly on the squared oilcloth in the bright, airy kitchen. She liked to hear all the news, and she always said, 'Well, fancy that now!'

I loved their house. It wasn't that I hated our own house, but Creaven's was so different. There was no loft in the kitchen, and there was a door high up in the wall opposite the fireplace, with no stairs. I had never seen it open. Anytime I had been in here I couldn't help staring at that brown door high up in the wall. It looked so shut off, so inaccessible. But it never made me afraid, as all other closed-up places did. I never felt fear in this house, with all its stillness and silences. It was as if, in a strange way that I couldn't explain, I belonged here.

My heart gave a jump inside me when I saw Hubert coming in the back door carrying a ladder.

'There's something I want to give you,' he said. He placed the ladder against the wall and climbed up. He took a key out of his waistcoat pocket and opened the door with a kind of reverence, as if he was the priest opening the tabernacle on the altar. He came down with a varnished box the size of a shoebox. It had a brass catch on the lid and four little windows made from perforated metal, like the windows of the meat-safe at home. He handed it to me.

'Keep your mayflies in this and they will have a better chance. At least their final hours will be happier.'

I was so shocked I didn't know what to say. Was he actually giving it to me? 'But is it for keeps, Mister Creaven?' I asked. 'I mean, why are you giving it to me? Where did it come from? It's beautiful.'

'I made it a long time ago, for . . . ' I heard the swish of the apron behind me and out of the corner of my eye I saw Mrs Creaven turn away towards the window and stare out over the fuchsia hedge at the deep blue lake. ' . . . for a small boy just like you. Now run along or your father will miss you.'

I was so excited that I nearly crashed into Doctor Maguire's car on the way back. For once I did not mind the work or the dust or my father's constant nagging about keeping the hay well spread out from under my feet. Every time I saw a green plantain leaf in the hay, I imagined it was a mayfly. I would pick it up and let it blow away on the wind as if it was alive.

We were just finishing the last meadow-cock when the skies opened. It rained solidly for four days. My father was all aglow with satisfaction but I was desperate. I felt like a prisoner as I stood in the doorway of the barn the following day, imagining that the streams of rain coming down from the galvanised roof were the bars of my cage. My father made a woolpack, stitching bags together with a packing needle while my brothers held the bags taut. The following day we mixed potash and ammonia in a great big heap on the barn floor, and my brothers had great fun breaking the lumps that rolled down the sides of the white, powdery mountain, but I was not interested. I just stood at the door, waiting for the rain to stop.

It seemed like an age afterwards when I parked my bicycle at the fuchsia hedge outside Creaven's and knocked on the door. The place was strangely silent. The rain dripped from the thatch onto the ivy leaves that flapped against the windowsill and there was a hollow sound from the waves that lapped against the black, perforated limestone rocks of the shore. Hubert's empty larch boat was tied to the rusty iron ring on the quay and it rocked and grated on the gravel like some big brown dog waiting for its owner to return. But there were no voices round the house. I pulled myself up by propping my elbows on the windowsill and looked in the front window, cupping my hands round my eyes to cut out the glare. The door high up on the wall was open, and the morning sun sent a shaft of light slanting down from the gable window through the gloomy interior and lit up the hearth, which would otherwise have been dark and lifeless.

I walked home, mystified, wheeling my bicycle and carrying the varnished box full of mayflies. Later, I sat in the hob by the fire while my mother tried to explain. As usual, she only half-told me things.

'Mister Creaven is not well,' she said. 'He's gone into a place called a sanatorium to get better. Sarah is gone to live with her sister in Hollymount. The poor woman has had a very sad life, God help her, and this is another terrible blow to her. Say a prayer for her when you are serving Mass.'

As soon as I could, I went up to the High Graffa by the hawthorn trees and opened the box and let the mayflies blow away to freedom. They all flew away easily. Their wings were strong and they were still green enough to blend with the leaves.

I never gathered mayflies again, but I kept the box on the window seat in my bedroom. I always kept the lid open, and every time I looked at it, it reminded me of an open door, high up in a wall.

THE SILVER DOLLAR

I managed to lift the big, heavy suitcase into the boot of the Morris Cowley even though I was only a puny ten years old. I was so excited I could have lifted the car itself. I was going to serve Mass at the Stations in Cloonkeely, the biggest village in the parish. There was always a collection for the priest and the altar boy at the stations, so it was a kind of testimonial, a pay-off for all the early mornings and the hassle of learning the Latin responses.

Earlier that morning, under the tetchy supervision of Canon Curley, the big case had been packed with altar stone and wine bottle, golden chalice and braided chasuble, Mass-book and bell and blessed candles. I had already put my own little brown case, with its starched and ironed surplice and long black soutane, into the back seat.

I stood outside the church in the misty morning and waited for the canon and the curate to appear from the sacristy. I felt really good. Across the road the grey hulk of Claran School loomed out of the fog. No school for me this morning. No worries about what kind of a mood Mrs O'Hanrahan was in. With any luck I would miss the dictation that we were supposed to have learned. No mental arithmetic either. I could do my own. Thirteen houses in Cloonkeely; probably eight at a shilling and five at sixpence. If it cost nine pence to get into the matinee in Todd Corbett's Hall, how many times could I go for ten and six? That was the kind of mental arithmetic I liked. The door of the sacristy opened before I could work out the answer, and the two priests emerged.

Father Hegarty, the curate, was tall and thin, with jet-black hair sleeked back straight from his forehead. He was only just out of the seminary, and he looked pale and undernourished. Canon Morgan was small and fat and grey-haired, with a round, red face. He looked as if he was always worried about something. He had been in the parish a long time. He knew everybody's history, and he expected people to jump to his command.

'Is everything in?' he asked sternly.

'Yes, canon,' I replied, hoping that nothing had been overlooked. I would get the blame if we forgot anything.

Soon we were gliding down country lanes, where the grass grew between the wheel-tracks and the longer tendrils of briar and hazel whipped off the windscreen. The leather upholstery was smooth against the backs of my knees and there was a faint smell of incense mingled with the stronger scent of pipe tobacco.

'Where are we off to today?' Father Hegarty asked, rubbing his hands and turning to wink at me. I liked him. He played football with us sometimes in the schoolyard.

'John Fahy's, down by the lake,' the canon replied, in his gruff voice. 'He's the one who paid the big price for the Kinsella's place, and he still has his Confirmation money to spend!'

'I think I know him,' the curate said. 'He never got married, did he?'

'Nobody would have a dowry good enough for him. But his sister Norah is home from America now. They say she's loaded.'

'Is she the one that married the . . . ?'

'You're very well up, for a blow-in,' the canon interrupted. 'She never came home, not even once, in forty years, until now.'

'Would you blame her?' Father Hegarty asked, half under his breath.

The canon gave no answer, but he did not seem too happy with that question. He just wiped the condensation off the windscreen and grunted.

I did not understand the conversation at all. It was the first time in my life I had heard a woman described as 'loaded'. I imagined a huge, fat woman, as big as a donkey, with two creels of turf on her back.

I slipped my hand into the leather loop that hung from above the window of the car, bracing myself against the turns and twists of the road and feeling my stomach left behind in mid-air whenever we shot over a little hill.

We made a sharp turn up an even narrower lane that twisted viciously for half a mile and suddenly came to what looked like a clearing in the hazel wood. The house was a low, thatched, whitewashed cottage, its window frames and door newly painted in bright red. There was a gravel path leading from the little garden gate down to a pier, which jutted out into the brooding lake. Small groups of men were gathered round the door, dressed in their Sunday clothes, and they doffed their caps as we passed in with the suitcases.

Inside, a bright ash fire crackled on the hearth and the smell of fresh paint and woodsmoke filled the warm kitchen. The big kitchen table had already been mounted on two chairs and covered in a crisp, white linen cloth to make a high altar.

Each of the two priests went into a room on either side of the kitchen to hear Confessions. I proceeded to unpack the altar stone and the candles and everything else in the order the canon wanted, all under the watchful eyes of the women who were seated around the walls. Opening my little case and donning the starched surplice, I felt as important as a doctor who had come to save a dying man, while the household looked on in awe. It was not the same as in the church. Here, in the confined space of the small kitchen, with people so close, the silence was compacted and condensed; there was no room for mistakes. Still, I managed a sweeping glance around the room to see if I could spot the fat woman, but there was no sign of anyone who might fit the description.

The men filed in and the Mass began. I kept my concentration, though the stone floor was hard on my knees. I rang the bell at the Consecration, and the Latin responses never bothered me. At last it was over and I could fix my attention on the money. The man of the house, as was the custom, put out the two chairs on the floor in front of the altar and Canon Morgan took out his red, dog-eared passbook.

'John Lee, Senior,' the canon intoned, standing behind the altar and looking out at the people over the top of his spectacles. There was an awkward silence before a stooped, bony old man shuffled forward and dropped a pound note on the priest's chair and a shilling on mine.

'John Lee, one pound,' the curate called from his position beside the chair. The canon marked it down.

'William Murphy.'

A short, stocky man with a weather-beaten face moved quickly forward, leading with his left shoulder, his head bowed and his eyes on the floor as if he was walking against a strong wind. Without once looking up, he slapped a ten-shilling note on the priests' chair as if it were the ace of trumps. He then threw sixpence on my chair before veering away and shouldering his way back into the crowd of men at the back door.

Each householder in turn came forward when his name was called and placed money on the chairs. Some paid a pound and some a ten-shilling note, and a shilling or sixpence for the clerk.

The priest was closing his notebook when she spoke from the parlour door – a loud, clear voice from another world. 'You don't have my name, Father, but I guess I'd like to make a contribution.' The voice cut into the cosiness of the kitchen like a cold blade, and when the silence returned, it tightened as if to try and heal the wound.

'The name's Norah Leroy.' There was a low murmur from the men at the back door, and the women around the fireplace exchanged darting glances. A tall, stately woman strode forward to the priests' chair. She was about sixty years old, with red lipstick, a black feather slanting out of her hat and a dead fox draped around her neck. She tossed a five-pound note on the priests' chair as if she was throwing a sweet to a child. A big, bright silver coin rattled on mine. It was like a half a crown, only bigger. The woman's face had a strange, satisfied look as she made her way back to the fireside, as if she had just settled an old score.

When the priest nodded in my direction, I gathered the coins from my chair and found among them a silver dollar, with a picture of an eagle on it and some Latin words that I could not pronounce. I forgot to count the rest of the money, I was so fascinated by the dollar's solid weight and roundness, turning it over and over in my hand.

The American lady joined her brother, the priests and me in the parlour afterwards for the customary breakfast of grapefruit segments, boiled eggs and toast. She was not shy, like the local women were when they talked to the priest. She talked confidently, like a teacher. She told us all about leaving for America in the 'twenties when was only sixteen, and how she could remember her mother and father crying as they stood on the little pier just down from the house and watched her board the steamer for Galway. She never saw them alive again, she said. She told the canon how she worked night and day, studying and nursing, and how she sent home as many dollars as she could.

'And your husband?' the canon asked, looking at her over the rim of his glasses. 'Wasn't it just last year that he . . . '

'He was the kindest man in the entire world that you could ever meet,' she interrupted quickly, as if she could not wait to tell us all about him.

'He was a paediatric surgeon in the hospital where I worked. He was from Cuba.'

Silence again; a different silence this time, as if that cold steel blade had finally touched a nerve.

You could see that Nora Leroy was not used to silence, that it was alien to her somehow. She looked straight at her brother, who was busy stirring his tea. She switched her steady gaze back to the canon before she spoke again quietly and evenly. 'You know, Father, my mother must have been praying awfully hard for me all those years. There must be about five million people in New York alone, people of all races and creeds, and yet out of all that many, I met the kindest, truest, most loving man in all the whole wide world.'

After she had finished speaking, she continued to look him straight in the eye as if it was a staring game. He finally lowered his eyes to the crumbs he was playing with on the white cloth and kept nodding his head silently.

On the way home in the car, I asked Father Hegarty what the words on the silver dollar meant.

'"In God We Trust" on the front . . . well, that's

easy enough. *"E Pluribus Unum"* on the back. That's Latin for "Out of Many, One." Would you like to swap it for a half a crown?' he asked. I knew he was only half joking. I think he was just trying to make conversation, because the canon was not in a talking mood.

'No thanks, Father,' I said, feeling the comfort of the heavy roundness of the silver dollar in my palm. 'I want to keep it.'

I thought of the words of Mrs Leroy at the breakfast table, about her meeting someone special out of many. *'E Pluribus Unum.'*

I kind of liked her. I felt she had given me a sort of history of her life, in a silver coin. And I was looking forward to searching for Cuba in the atlas when I got back to school.

TODD CORBETT'S PICTURE HOUSE

I had just made my First Holy Communion. I had done exceptionally well, according to my mother. One of the things that impressed her was that I arrived all the way home from my First Confession with my hands still firmly joined. She should have known that this was because Mrs O'Kelly had instilled such fear in us that we were joining our hands and genuflecting at the drop of a hat. In any event, I looked so holy that my sister, Rose, was commissioned to bring me to the pictures as a reward.

The only film I had ever seen was at school when the travelling show came, and we were treated to some film about Saint Bernadette. The sound system worked so badly that we were not sure whether the film was in English or French, and the school windows were not darkened properly, so the sun blotted out half the picture. By all accounts, it would be nothing compared to the cinema, with its red, upholstered seats and its delicious darkness shutting out all the distractions of the real world.

From the little dog-eared programme of forthcoming

attractions, I picked what I felt would be a rip-roaring western. It was called 'Son of a Paleface' and starred Bob Hope, Bing Crosby and Jane Russell.

Of course I knew that Rose hated bringing me. She was eighteen at the time. She wore dirndl skirts that came in a parcel from America and bright red lipstick whenever she went to a dance in the town hall, so she felt far too sophisticated to be bringing her little brother on the carrier of a bicycle into town to the pictures.

The cinema in Headford didn't have a grandiose name like 'The Palace' or 'The Luxor'. It was just called 'Todd Corbett's Hall', after the enterprising citizen who had established it. The parish priest looked on it as a den of iniquity and predicted that the place would end up as a cow-byre. He sometimes went along as censor, sitting under the projector window and holding up his hat to block out any unsavoury material that the man in Harcourt Street might have missed.

On that momentous night of my first visit, the crowd had gathered but the lights were still up and the show had not yet started by the time my sister ushered me into the hall and paid my one and sixpence. I can still hear the low, expectant murmur, and the mingled smell of musty overcoats and perfume comes back to me as if it were yesterday. I can see the orange glow from the lights along the side walls and there, at the top of the room, the silver screen, big and bright and spotless, like some god that we had come to adore.

I followed my sister slowly, mesmerised by the wonder and awesomeness of it all, and then, before

188

going into my seat, in full view of the gathered throng, I genuflected! Yes, I bent my knee low in reverence to Hollywood, right down to the floor, as I had been programmed to do in chapel. I had just finished blessing myself when I realised that I had earned a crescendo of laughter and a resounding round of applause. My sister was mortified and did not speak to me for three solid weeks. In her skilful way she made me feel like a fool and in my childish nightmares I was tied to a totem pole while she attacked me with a tomahawk.

Forty years have gone by in the history of the cinema since that night. Recently I went back to find that Todd Corbett's Hall is, in fact, a cattle-shed beside the mart. I have seen many films, most of which I have long forgotten, but I will never forget 'Son of a Paleface', and I feel a certain unease every time I go into a cinema. I hesitate before taking my place and sometimes I imagine I hear a little trickle of applause.

Every mind makes its own flashbacks and the editors of memory cut their own scenes.

LENT IN THE GREEN VALLEY

I don't know why the sight of a bunch of daffodils dancing at the trunk of a tree reminded me of Lent. Maybe there was a sweet smell on the breeze that made them dance. I suppose the keys of memory have subtle notches in them and there is no telling how they work.

When spring came to the green valley that was our childhood in the west of Ireland, the daffodils danced and the primroses bloomed and from Ash Wednesday our talk was of fasting from sweets. We saved them and hid them for forty days of what was supposed to be abstinence but was really gluttony delayed.

Our taste in those days of wonder was limited, bound by poverty perhaps, but enriched by rarity. Our culinary year was highlighted by cake at Christmas, eggs at Easter, stolen apples in September and satchels full of nuts from the hazel wood in Carnacrow when the brown leaves began to curl and wither.

But Lent was a special time when my brothers and I, for our imagined sins, were to save up our sweets. It was a time to find a biscuit tin in which we could hoard our forbidden fruit. We counted and compared num-

*Of this day for all the intentions of thy Sacred
     Heart
And for the intentions of our Holy Father, the
     Pope.*

That meant that you couldn't really do anything bad
that day, because how could you offer up something
bad for the intentions of the Sacred Heart? It also meant
that if you hit your thumb with a hammer, you didn't
curse, but you offered up the pain to God for all the
sins you had committed. What was it compared to the
pain Jesus had suffered on the cross? My mother would
exhort in her own gentle, comforting way if we skinned
a knee or cut a finger: 'Offer it up, offer it up.'

The guardian angel saved you from big danger.
Cutting a finger was minor stuff; but if you were
walking by a sheer cliff, your guardian angel would
keep you back from the edge and catch you if you
should stumble and were about to plunge to your death:

*O Angel of God, my Guardian dear,
To whom God's love commits me here,
Ever this day be at my side
To light and guard, to rule and guide.
              Amen.*

Every time we left the house, we dipped our finger in
the holy-water font inside the door and blesse
ourselves. My mother replenished the holy wა
faithfully from the baptismal font in the church.
however, when my father dipped his finger in f

bers of Cleeve's Toffee and Peggy's Legs and Bulls' Eyes.
You could buy twelve NKMs in Ellie Fallon's for a penny.
The letters stood for 'North Kerry Manufacture', I think,
but we thought they meant 'Nicest Kind Made'. There
were black bars that we called 'Cough No Mores'. The
tin box in which they came captured a sweet smell, a
dazzling display of decadence, and a delayed indulgence that would come to a sickening climax at
Easter.

For our older sisters, too, Lent was a time when
they wandered through their own particular wasteland.
For them it was a desert without dances. There were
no station parties, no capers down to Cong or to the
town hall in Tourmakeady, no quicksteps or slow
foxtrots to Mick Delahunty and his Orchestra.

But one year, in that Lent-time of social deprivation,
they were visited on Sunday evenings by two harbingers
of hope. Two men came courting to our thatched house
in the green valley. They cycled in the lane by the rows
of daffodils and parked their bicycles at the turf-shed
and came in to pay their restrained respects. They had
Windsor knots in their ties and their polished shoes
shone in the light of the fire.

And they always brought sweets for us children.
The older man, who was fat, brought Rum and Butter,
and the younger one, a dapper little man with a
moustache, always brought a quarter-pound of Yorkshire Toffee. And so we named them after their gifts.

Being the youngest and most indiscreet in the house,
I once ventured to curry favour with these Sunday-
night visitors by showing them my treasure trove,

which had been stowed under a loose floorboard in our bedroom.

'Where do you hide them?' Rum and Butter asked.

'Down a hole upstairs,' I divulged, at which remark my mother, God rest her soul, turned as scarlet as the raspberry halfpenny bar in my gleaming silver box.

'My God!' she remonstrated when they had left. 'What made you say that? They must think this place is falling apart.'

Whether it was that they distrusted the carpentry in our house or that their passion eventually cooled, I will never know, but the once-regular visits of Rum and Butter and Yorkshire Toffee petered out – much to our disappointment.

But we toasted them that Easter Sunday long ago and savoured their blessed generosity, and though they have long since passed on I savour their memory now. They peopled that simple time in our lives when sweets were a wonder and innocence danced with the daffodils.

FAITH OF OUR FATHERS

Faith of our fathers, living still
In spite of dungeon, fire and sword;
Oh, how our hearts beat high with joy
Whene'er we hear that glorious word!

When we were growing up, the Catholic faith c[o] through our veins like our life's blood. We were the fear of hell, the pain of guilt, the suddenn death and the length of eternity. We were con reminded that God was all around us, and He missed a thing. From the time when we open eyes in the morning until we closed them at ni guided and determined everything and we had thank for it. We were on our knees first thing our prayers, and that meant two prayers: the M Offering and the prayer to our guardian angel

O Jesus, through the most pure heart of Ma
I offer you all my prayers, works and suffer

and found it dry as a bone, he blessed himself with the words: 'The devil damn the drop ever in it!'

We wouldn't dare to sit down and eat before first bowing our heads and saying the Grace Before Meals. If we finished and rose to go without reciting the Grace After Meals, we were castigated as savages. When the Angelus rang out across the fields from Claran Church at noon and again at six in the evening, everybody blessed themselves and bowed their heads in prayer. Everything stopped. If you were leading a horse and cart out of the boreen, you stopped and waited until the peals of the bell died away. The horse shook its harness and work resumed.

At night when the supper dishes had been cleared away, the Rosary beads were taken down from the beam. Each of us had our own beads in its own little purse. Sometimes they were broken and repaired again with wire. The chairs were all turned towards the picture of the Sacred Heart and we knelt on the stone floor and said the five decades:

> *Thou, O Lord wilt open my lips.*
> *And my tongue shall announce Thy praise.*

My father would say the first decade, my mother the second, and so on in descending order from oldest to youngest child. I never got to say a decade until I was almost old enough to vote. It wasn't fair, but maybe it was just as well, because it was an awesome re-sponsibility. You had to be deadly accurate in the way you said the Hail Mary and, most of all, you had to count properly to the 'Glory be to the Father'. One slip of the tongue and you set everybody into fits of suppressed laughter. Sometimes we deliberately set each other laughing. During the long Litany that was always said at the end of the Rosary, when everybody was responding, 'Pray for us', someone would whisper 'Make tay for us', and we would hold our noses in concealed, infectious laughter.

We would not even dream of tumbling into bed without first kneeling to say our personal night prayers:

> *Night has fallen, dear Mother, the long day is*
> *   o'er,*
> *And before your loved image I'm kneeling once*
> *   more*
> *To thank you for keeping me safe through the*
> *   day;*
> *To ask you this night to keep evil away.*

You had to say the Act of Contrition and mean it, or you might die in your sleep, and where would you be then? You had to force sincerity on yourself, making several runs at it. Sometimes the enormity of an imagined sin would get the better of you and you would toss and turn all night in restless anxiety, falling, falling into a furnace that had opened under a crack in the earth.

Our weeks and months were bounded by religion, our year mapped by the Church calendar. On Saturdays at twelve noon, we younger ones washed our hands and faces and trooped to Confession. We sat in a row in the cool, shadowed silence amid the smell of candle-wax and furniture polish, boys on one side of the confessional, girls on the other, watching our friends troop in from the farms around, some pattering in bare feet on the cool chapel floor, others clumping down the aisle in noisy hobnail boots. We would all kneel in unison when the parish priest appeared, his red face set in a serious frown as he removed his biretta. We would file in one by one into the darkness.

'Bless me Father, for I have sinned,' we would say then.

'How long since your last confession?'

'A fortnight, Father.'

'Tell me your sins.'

'I cursed. I told lies.'

Everybody had the same sins.

We could hear everything clearly as we sat in silence, looking at the initials scratched on the pews, wondering whether 'M.W.' was Michael Walsh in Annaghkeen or Martin Walsh in Knocklahard. You could never be sure. The corncrake droned away in the meadow outside and the sins droned in the echoing church.

'For your penance, say three Our Fathers and three Hail Marys.'

Everybody's penance was the same as well.

Finally we escaped into the glare of the day. We hung around to argue for a while about how many bird's nests we had found, to call the girls names, and to throw a few stones at the school.

On Sunday we went to Mass in the morning and Benediction in the evening. We children were hustled out to the church first, all scrubbed and dressed in our Sunday best, with our hair parted and sleeked, our socks with tops turned down, and our shoes polished. We were warned to sit up at the top of the nave with all the other children: boys on the right-hand side of the aisle, with their short pants and sleeked hair, girls on the left, all style, in floral dresses with huge ribbons in their hair. We all carried a prayer book and Rosary beads. The girls' prayer books were full of little 'holy pictures' that they exchanged whenever there was a mission in the parish: 'Always remember Margaret Lee, April 1946.' If you were lucky you might have an 'In Memoriam' card, with a picture of some dead relative that you had never seen: 'Pray for Michael Molloy, Curramore.' He looked out at you with doleful eyes, not knowing that his look would be trapped in time. You studied the picture and wondered about death and eternity and heaven and hell. I had a picture of Dominic Savio, because I was in the Dominic Savio Club. I had the badge as well. I wanted to be like him, to have that same look of piety that I saw on his face in the picture in my prayer book. My Sunday-morning daydreams saw me dying young, heroic, in my mother's arms, as she wept and I comforted her, telling her that I would bring her safely to heaven with me one day.

My father always walked to Mass alone, striding stately and tall past his straight drills of potatoes and his tidy fields with his starched collar and tie and his new-pressed suit. Except for Sodality Sundays, he sat at the end of the last seat in the side aisle. I can see him now, shoulders back, his thick shock of silvery hair, his bright eyes glinting and playful, his lips drawn into a thin smile of satisfaction. He liked Sundays: it was the end of the week and the work was done. Now he could sit at the head of the seat where he always sat and adopt that look of someone who had earned the right to be respected and admired. When he got home he could joke about someone he had seen at Mass whose drills were as crooked as a bag of teapots.

My mother was always the last to leave the house for Mass. She had to make sure everybody was looked after, the fire was safe and the door was closed. She prayed fervently and piously in the church, her bowed head tilted slightly, her lips moving constantly. Every now and then she would raise the cross of her beads to her lips and kiss it fervently. She had a huge missal, full of 'In Memoriam' cards and pictures that smiled out at her, as if, like all the rest of us, they knew they could rely on her to the end.

At six o' clock every Sunday evening we trooped to Benediction. We sat in the slanting dusty sunbeams of the church and recited the five decades of the Rosary, the hard wood of the kneelers biting into our bare knees. Then the priest and servers left the altar and the birdsong from the yew trees outside infiltrated through the open door. The priest re-emerged, all pomp and ceremony, his shoulders draped in the golden-braided amice, which he used to shield his grip on the silver monstrance. The choir of girls from the organ loft burst into:

O Salutaris hostia
quae caeli pandis ostium

The thurible jingled and the sweet blue incense smoke rose into the evening air, catching the shafts of coloured light that poured through the stained-glass windows. The golden doors of the tabernacle were unlocked and the pyx inserted into the centre of the monstrance, which looked like an old drawing of the sun. The server rang the bell furiously and then the priest swung the silver image of the sun in front of us all three times and we looked once and then bowed our heads and closed our eyes because we were not worthy to see any more. The gold and silver orb flickered and shimmered and shone inside our closed eyelids as the choir chanted:

Tantum ergo Sacramentum
veneremur cernui:
et antiquum documentum
novo cedat ritui;
praestet fides suplementum
sensuum defectui

The words of Aquinas were known but not understood, but then the mystery was the magic of it all – the mystery is what was shown to us in those quiet evenings in that sheltered church among the meadows of the green valley while the birds sang and the cows moved slowly homewards to be milked. We did not ask for more.

The Church shaped our year and marked the milestones on it, from the fasting of Lent to the ceremonies at Easter, and on to Rogation days, Ascension Thursday, Corpus Christi, the harvest collection, the Stations in the village twice a year, All Saints' Day, All Souls' Day and the great feast of Christmas to brighten the winter's gloom.

During Lent the Redemptorists came to preach the mission and purge us of our complacent ways. They were fiery men, with eyes and gestures and words that held us captive in the packed church and stirred our souls into a burning fever. They wagged their fingers at us and shook their heads in despair at our floundering faith. They told dramatic stories about people on their deathbeds. Why do fragments of these old stories hang still in my memory like a torn cloth on a bush? The priest had been visiting a house with another missionary, a man older and wiser than himself. They enquired about the welfare of the family within. The mother spoke of their good fortune: the children were all healthy and happy. Their business was thriving. No sickness or affliction had ever befallen them. A cloud passed over the older missionary's face. He rose and shook his cassock, saying, 'Let us flee this house that God has never blessed with the shadow of a cross!'

When these stories were told, the voice of the missionary would rise to a crescendo and then fall to a hushed whisper. He would pause for a second or two to let the message sink in. 'Let us flee this house that God has never blessed with the shadow of a cross.' He repeated the punchline, swept his glasses from his eyes and looked around the church, staring into every eye at once. We gazed up at him through a ring of candlelight, spellbound, transfixed, afraid to breathe. He held us in the palm of his hand. Our own poor pastor, confined to the sacristy, must have felt his stock diminish to an all-time low.

The people filed out of the church filled with zeal, ready to shoulder any burden. The canvas stalls did a roaring trade in statues that glowed in the dark, holy pictures, holy-water fonts, brown scapulars, green scapulars, Rosary beads, prayer books, crucifixes, little plastic cameras that showed you pictures of Knock when you clicked the button, and little blue domes that snowed on Our Lady after you turned them upside down. On the last night of the mission, people brought their holy objects to be blessed. There was a man from Loggawannia who held up his child to give him a better view, just as the priest was asking the people to hold up their holy objects to be blessed. From that day on, the unfortunate child grew up with the nickname 'The Holy Object'. One of the last ceremonies of mission week was the Renunciation of Satan.

'Do you renounce Satan?'

'We do.'

'And all his works?'

'We do.'

The missionary was not satisfied with the level of response. 'That's no way to show your commitment! You couldn't hear that behind a wet newspaper. The devil is certainly not going to hear it. This time, shout it out like you mean it!'

There was a simple man called Mártan, half-mad with *poitín,* who lived alone on the edge of the bog at Ballinacregg. I suppose he must have felt the need for special protection from Ould Nick. He was getting louder than anybody else in his denunciation of Satan. The priest went for the final, resounding run.

'Do you renounce Satan?'

'To hell with him, the bastard!' Mártan shouted from the back of the church, his fist clenched in frenzy.

Corpus Christi was a day we looked forward to for weeks. We were allowed to go to the procession in Headford and, best of all, we had saved our pennies for ages and we could spend them now. The priest in all his robes walked through the newly painted town, holding the monstrance high. Men in sashes held a canopy with golden tassels over his head. Girls in white Communion dresses walked backwards in front of them, picking rose petals out of baskets, kissing them and strewing them on the ground in front of the priest. Children of Mary, in blue sashes and white veils, walked next, then the choir, singing loud enough to be heard all the way back to the end of the winding skein of people behind them:

Hail, Queen of Heav'n, the ocean star,
Guide of the wand'rer here below:
Thrown on life's surge, we claim thy care,
Save us from peril and from woe.

Mother of Christ, star of the sea,
Pray for the wand'rer, pray for me.

Every shopfront was decorated for the occasion: each one had an altar in the window – the Child of Prague, the Sacred Heart, Saint Martin de Porres. There was bunting across the street and festivity in the air. Not a car passed, not a horn sounded, not a ring of a till or a shop bell was heard, only the crunch of soles on the gravel of the street and the words of the choir wafting on the breeze:

Bring flowers of the fairest,
Bring blossoms the rarest
From garden and hillside and woodland and
    dale.
Our full hearts are swelling,
Our glad voices telling
The praise of the loveliest flower of the vale.

When the procession was over, the shops opened and we bought wafers of ice cream and Peggy's Legs and a bottle of lemonade or Corrib Orange if we could afford it. Truth to tell, that was the high point for us – the reason we looked forward to this day and counted the hours and the pennies in anticipation of its coming. Our days ran and were counted between events like these. We trudged the three miles home from the painted town, our white plimsolls grey with the dust of the sandy roads, our white shirts maybe with a yellow blob or two of lemonade on them, our hearts heavy that it was all over for another year.

Our lives were lived in the porch and portal of the life to come: everything that happened had a reason that we did not understand, but God did. 'Welcome be the will of God,' the old people said. 'Amen to that,' was the answer. There was an acceptance of suffering, a resignation to the great plan of our creation that we did not understand, or try to. If a child died, then God wanted her more than her parents did. If a man or woman went crazy, then they were a *Duine le Dia,* a person of God. The souls of the faithful departed walked beside us on the road and knew our every struggle. Some of them were in purgatory, suffering for maybe a thousand years for just a venial sin. Every year, on All Souls' Day, we made a concerted and determined effort to get them out, because we knew that if we did, then they would do the same for us when they had the ear of God in heaven. Each time you visited the church on that special day only, and said five Our Fathers and five Hail Marys and five Glories for the souls of the faithful departed, you earned a plenary indulgence on their behalf. That meant that a soul went straight to heaven each time. But you had to leave the church before you began the next visit. There was a constant coming and going. People went out the door to the steps of the church, had a little chat with a supplicant neighbour and went back in to the church to start again. The souls flew out of purgatory. We children made sure we left the church each time. We ran round the church, chased the girls in the darkness of yew trees and tombstones, felt for the first time the softness of femininity and the surge of desire. Then we returned to the candlelit church to free another soul such as ours from the shackles that bound them.

When my eldest sister Mary was about eight, her eyes were slightly cast. It was so slight that nobody really noticed, but Aunt Mollie said it was not good and should be cured. On a cloudy Sunday afternoon in May, when the hawthorn blossoms were snowing in the laneways, Molly put on her shawl, took the child by the hand and led her to Tobar Ciaráin, a broken circle of stones overhung by trees, with dark water at the bottom of the steps. She took the five white pebble-stones that rested in the little font by the entrance and used them to count her five prayerful laps of the well, dropping one back into the niche each time. Then she bathed the child's eyes with the water. She left a little broken statue in a niche in the wall, along with all the other tributes that people before her had left: old beads, crucifixes, medals now turning green inside little stitched pouches. Leave something. Leave your ailment and your cross. Leave the path round the well worn and trampled with trouble, the walls full of signs of hope springing as eternal as the water within.

The God that we believed in was a counting God. Novenas lasted for nine First Fridays; there were Ten Commandments, Seven Deadly Sins, Seven Gifts of the Holy Ghost, fifteen Mysteries of the Rosary and fourteen Stations of the Cross. We young ones were given a penance of three Our Fathers and three Hail Marys for our sins, but we had heard of people whose sins were so awful that they got the full fifteen Mysteries of the Rosary. And had we not heard, too, of people who turned out to be insane criminals, and that was because the priest had omitted some word from the ritual when he was baptising them?

For some, their God was an old God, rooted in the old ways that linked with the sun and moon and the turn of the year. On May Day, Mary Kate Mannion always tied a branch of the mountain ash tree to the churn to prevent the milk from being stolen, and Máirtín Seán twisted a limb of hawthorn round the door of the byre before the cows were driven out to pasture so that their udders would not dry up. There were people my father pointed out to us who had got lost at night, coming home from a game of cards. What had happened was quite simple. They had stepped on the *fóidín mearbhaill,* the 'stray sod', and were carried hither and thither, unknown to themselves, until they were dizzy and disorientated. The only thing that rescued them – and lucky for them that they knew it – was that they turned their jacket inside out. Then they recovered their senses. You could be unlucky enough to step on the *féar gortach,* the 'hungry grass', and get so famished with the hunger that you fell down, and yet would not be able to eat a thing.

Sometimes the souls of the faithful departed got a little too close for comfort. My father told us solemnly and dramatically about the night he walked home alone from Headford, and as he passed Ellagh, just in sight of the graveyard, a woman appeared beside him, walking noiselessly, never speaking. Whenever he told us the story, a shiver tingled our backs and our mouths dried up with fear. Sometimes he refused to tell the story, because my mother would blame him for frightening us. That made us believe it all the more. But my mother had a story that frightened us even more. One night when her mother – my grandmother – was sewing by the fire late at night, the latch was lifted and the back door opened, though nobody was there. She thought it must have been the wind. It was five past two by the clock on the wall. The following night, as she sewed by the fire, the back door opened again. She looked at the clock. It was precisely five past two. She was so frightened she walked backwards out of the kitchen all the way past the door, never taking her eyes off it, transfixed with fear. She never stayed up late at night again.

There was an incident closer to home that was authenticated and is still believed. One night, at 3 am, three distinct knocks were heard in the empty parlour directly underneath the girls' bedroom. My sister Cecile heard them first; they sounded as if someone was knocking on the ceiling. She was the least credulous of us all. My father also heard them: three loud knocks on the door of his consciousness. He got up and found no one there. They told the story at breakfast. 'Someone is dead,' Molly said, blessing herself. Sure enough, the word came that morning: my father's cousin had died in his sleep.

And so our sleeping time was fretful and full of fearful dreams. We looked for the shield of God to guard us and closed our eyes to shut out the pitch darkness that might reveal a light at the window. We tried desperately not to hear the mysterious knocks that sounded in the dead of night when we awoke from a chasing nightmare. We covered our heads with the bedclothes and said five Our Fathers and five Hail Marys for the poor souls. It had to be five. Four was no good. Go back if you're not sure. And don't forget the Act of Contrition. And you had better mean it.

'I will never chase the girls again under the yew trees,' I said to myself. 'Oh God, I'm going straight to hell!'

The Old Master

After three years of laissez-faire education, I graduated into the master's room. Tommy Garvey was getting old by then and had lost some of his sharpness, but he was still a marvellous teacher and only very seldom had to reach for the cane. Every single day at five past three he passed our fields on his bicycle to Headford, where he sat alone in the snug of McCormacks' Hotel and drank two pints of porter and two half-whiskeys. He was a small man who wore a topcoat and a hard hat to school; then he peeled off to his waistcoat and shirtsleeves and raced round the room like a whirling dervish.

He taught as if he was running out of time, as if we had only this chance to learn and no other. He had maps of the world with magical place names like Abyssinia and Wagga Wagga, and he spoke about them as if he had been there. He held us spellbound with stories from history like the victory of Brian Boru at Clontarf, the escape of Art Ó Néill from Dublin Castle, the military exploits of Patrick Sarsfield and the great oratory of Daniel O'Connell. He laced the history with

the great magisterial poems of Aubrey de Vere and Sir
Samuel Ferguson:

> *O'er many a river bridged with ice,*
> *Through many a vale with snowdrifts dumb,*
> *Past quaking fen and precipice*
> *The Princes of the North are come!*

> *Lo, these are they that year by year*
> *Roll'd back the tide of England's war.*
> *Rejoice, Kinsale! Thy help is near!*
> *That wondrous winter march is o'er.'*

He was an entertainer, an actor, and he put every ounce
of energy into the day's teaching from the moment we
entered the room in the morning until the bell rang at
three o'clock. We could never relax, because he would
not let us. He taught algebra and geometry and
trigonometry. We worked in acres, roods and perches;
pounds, hundredweights and tons; gallons, quarts and
pints. He gave us the most complex mathematical
problems and talked us through them, and when we
arrived at the answer he made us feel a sense of
accomplishment, a pride in ourselves. He loved sums
where you used the unitary method: 'Half a ton of
potatoes can be bought for £5/12s/6d. How many
hundredweight can be bought for £13/10s/0d at this
rate?'

He brought us into the fields and laneways beside
the school and gave us the names of the wild flowers
and grasses, some of which we might have known only

in Irish: butterwort and cranesbill, dog rose and robin-run-the-hedge. We gathered samples and pressed them in a book. He introduced us to the elements of science and horticulture, soil analysis and crop rotation. It was as if he felt a great urgency to open as many windows in our raw minds as he could, as if this was the only chance we would ever get. Indeed, up to that time, very few progressed into secondary education. This would be the end of the line. You left school at fourteen and made your own way in the world. Only the children of the shopkeeper in the town or of the schoolmaster himself could go to boarding school. But Tommy Garvey sent us out to the great dome of the world as ready as any child could be.

The Old Master, as we used to call him, hated examinations: they were alien to his philosophy of education. He had to deal with two: Confirmation and the Primary Certificate. The Primary Cert consisted of three examination papers sent out from the Department of Education in July: English, Irish and arithmetic. We had to write a composition, parse and analyse a sentence and answer one or two questions in grammar. The arithmetic examination was made up of two parts: problems and mental arithmetic. 'How many 1/2d stamps could I buy for £1/6s/8d?' The local principals swapped schools for the day of the exam, but they always helped you out on the day if you were stuck. Even so, some unfortunates managed to fail the examination, and when word got out, they were shamed forever, and the whisper 'He didn't even pass the Primary Cert' dogged them like a curse for the rest of their lives.

A Strong and Perfect Christian

Confirmation held out the prospect of even greater humiliation. Up at the altar-rails, in front of the whole neighbourhood and the bishop himself, you faced your defining moment. You answered a catechism question at the top of your voice while the world around you stood still and held its breath. If you got it right, the catechism said you became 'a strong and perfect Christian'.

I was in Fifth Class, decked out in a wine blazer my sister Mary had bought in Clery's. And I wore my first long trousers. Presents of beads and prayer books and scapulars and medals had rained down on me from aunts and uncles I had hardly even heard of. We had practiced Catechism, Bible history, Catechism notes and every possible twist and turn of our religious knowledge at school for weeks on end, until I felt that I knew as much as the priest himself.

The church was packed to the rafters, full of the pomp and ceremony of the braided bishop in his mitre and staff. Triumphant hymns shook the walls; incense hung like ether in the perspiring air. Pale, starched schoolchildren trembled like jelly. Someone passed out and fell, a head full of Catechism cracking the floor like a coconut. Some children were examined by the priests, who flitted about like flies. A rumour went round the seats like a breeze that the bishop would examine only the Sixth Class. I was devastated. How could I show off my knowledge now? It was all very disappointing.

A lithe, bony-faced priest with sleek, oiled hair swooped on our seat. 'I think we have to go up to the bishop, Father,' I said timidly, not wanting him to make a mistake.

'Oh, really?' he replied sarcastically. 'Am I not good enough for you?'

The way he said 'good' made me fell as small as a three-penny bit. I lowered my head in respectful humility.

He let the silence hang like a judgement in the air. 'What is presumption?' he snapped, fixing me with a cold stare.

I stared back at him, frozen with a cold fear. He was bent over me, his face so close that I could tell he had had a boiled egg for breakfast. 'Well?' he persisted.

I was flattened. My mind was blank as a slate, all the tangled weave of learned answers gone like a cobweb in a stream. It was different when the master asked the questions. I could rattle off the answers like clockwork. Perspiration oozed out of my forehead and my new shirt collar tightened like a noose.

The priest straightened up to look at the Sixth Class trooping up to the bishop. 'Just as well you're not going up there to make a fool of yourself,' he said archly.

Then someone behind me whispered the word 'False'. I was off like a hare, blurting out the answer like a kettle boiling over: 'Presumption is a false expectation of salvation without making proper use of the necessary means to obtain it.'

'And don't you forget it, sonny,' the priest said, pointing his finger like a gun at the centre of my forehead.

When he was gone, I turned around to find out who had rescued me from the dead. It was Veronica Toole, the shopkeeper's daughter. She sat there with her golden ringlets and her white veil like a vision of the Virgin Mary. She lowered her beautiful blue eyes and smiled shyly, and from that blessed moment on I was confirmed a weak and imperfect Christian. On my way down from the altar, having had my cheek stroked by the bishop, I saw only her among the blurred, hazy throng that packed the church. I swaggered home in my long trousers and wine blazer intoxicated with the smell of the new-mown hay, my mind racing ahead like thistledown on the warm summer breeze. Sitting in the Old Master's classroom, across from the girls, across from Veronica Toole, would never, ever be the same again.

BIRTHS

The girls in our family in the green valley were, as I said, somewhat older than us boys. They moved to a different rhythm, talked about different things, laughed at things we did not understand. When I was still in short pants, Cecile, Una and Rose were in their early teens. They plucked petals from daisies and found that it told them if someone loved them. Whenever they peeled an apple, they peeled it in one long, unbroken skein, so that when they threw it over their shoulder it spelt the initials of their sweetheart. They went for endless walks along the road and talked to young men who happened to come by on bicycles. They read *Woman's Weekly* and listened to *Mrs Dale's Diary* on the BBC Light Programme. They crooned songs sung by Perry Como and Frankie Lane. Whenever they went to a Station party or a dance, they smelt of lavender and repaired runs in their stockings with blobs of nail varnish.

Their best friend, Maggie, lived behind the crossroads. You could see her house through the trees, halfway between our house and the church. She had four brothers, all older that her. She came skipping over to visit and chat and sing and help with tying the corn too when the young men were around. She was a bubbly sixteen-year-old, with dark, curly hair, a round face and eyes as brown as a hazelnut. She was lithe and tawny and full of energy, hopping about like a cat, drawing in the dust with the toe of her shoe, combing back her hair with her fingers, forever chewing a wisp of grass or blowing out a dandelion clock. She never stood still.

My father watched over our girls like a hawk. If they were late home from a party or a dance, he was up waiting for them in the kitchen and there would be hell to pay. He had my brother Pat look out for them, even though he was slightly younger than they were. He was to report on whom they were with and where they went. He was never to arrive home without them. Once, when he stole in quietly at two in the morning minus the girls, my father was at the door, livid with rage, to confront him. Pat gave the excuse that Cecile's bicycle had got punctured and the rest were walking with her. The old man did not buy that for a minute, and when they did arrive home he bellowed so loudly at them that he woke up the whole house. They were not allowed out again for weeks, until my mother pleaded on their behalf.

What delayed them on those stolen nights was innocent enough. A furtive kiss and cuddle behind the gable of the town hall, or maybe a walk homewards, holding hands with a man, their giggling companions a few steps behind. They had been warned often enough about dark, leafy laneways as 'occasions of sin'. They knew what lusty country youths were like.

They seldom went on those expeditions without Maggie being with them. She was the life and soul of the dance. She made fun of the men and their serious ways. She teased and mimicked them and laughed at their shyness and frustrations.

On a balmy Sunday evening in August, the girls made their way back to the church for Benediction. My brothers and I followed closely behind, listening to their silly talk. 'Are my seams straight?' Maggie asked, straightening her leg and trying to look at the line of her stockings at the back.

We jeered loudly and mimicked her, pulling up the leg of our pants. It was just another normal Sunday evening. After Benediction, the girls chatted and laughed outside Maggie's house and then ran home. There was no dancing that night.

Next morning there seemed to be a commotion at Maggie's house. The doctor's car had arrived. Then Maggie's father went on his bicycle to the priest's house. The priest arrived. My mother put on her *binneog* and went back to the house, thinking that someone had died. She was gone for quite a while. When she came back home she was shaking her head, an incredulous look on her face. My father looked at her and knew something was wrong.

We boys were put out into the scullery, as usual. We strained our ears at the cross-door.

'Maggie's just had a baby girl,' my mother kept saying. 'Maggie's just had a baby girl.'

The girls were called down from their room.

'Did you know about this and not say a word to anybody?' she asked them

'No, we did not. No!'

'Who did she go with?'

'She didn't go with anybody that we knew about.'

'Honestly, we didn't know a thing!'

'We were with her at the Rosary yesterday, and she never said a thing.' Rose began to cry bitterly. 'We didn't know a thing.'

And neither did they, and I don't know if Maggie knew a thing either. Some time later, we saw a strange car arrive at their house, and a strange man went in. Maggie got married a few weeks later, to a man from Cong. Our girls never met her again until years later. She lived, happily or not, and reared her daughter and four more sons. The girls missed her, and felt as though there was some kind of a betrayal on someone's part.

There was a story told about another birth. Though the story would not have been told in our hearing, we picked it up piecemeal. It was something that happened not long before I was born. Over beyond the Cahermór crossroads lived the Freeneys. There were three girls in the family, and two boys. Their father kept an Aberdeen Angus bull. Neighbouring farmers, in those days before artificial insemination, brought their cows to be serviced by the bull. The daughters were always on hand to help prepare the cow for the bull if the man of the house or his sons were away in the fields. They would laugh and joke and banter with the men while nature took its course before their eyes in the paddock. The men would always return home with their cows and remark what fine daughters Mike Freeney had.

The eldest Freeney girl had a baby out of wedlock and shortly afterwards the youngest girl took sick and died suddenly, after a very short illness. There was talk among the neighbours that she, too, had had a baby, but none was found, even though the police came and searched the premises, dug up the garden and even opened the coffin. The old women whispered and the men nodded and the rumour stayed. Those girls were too exposed to nature, people said. They should have been sheltered from it.

Such events were rare, it must be said, and made the news for that reason. Most births happened within the family, at home, with Nurse Kelly in attendance. She was a busy woman. Seldom would a doctor be called to deliver a baby, unless there were complications. The babies came, plentifully, and were accepted and cherished. Most families were large – some, very large. There was a family of fifteen, who found it hard to survive. The boys often came over to our house to play. My mother always made them sit down at table with us and have a hearty meal. They all survived and seemed to be happy.

We heard of only one baby, born the eldest of a family, who was not welcome. When Nurse Kelly presented the baby girl to the mother, the mother turned her head away. 'A girl! What do I want with a girl? What good is a girl to us?' she said. She wanted a son to leave the farm to, to do the ploughing, the harrowing and the reaping, she said. She was angry. It was as if she blamed the nurse for the outcome of her labour. She never did have a son. The farm was left to a nephew when the parents died. The unwanted daughter grew up to be a surgeon.

Sometimes a child would have been welcome but none was born. Michael Canavan was a great friend of the parish priest, until they fell out. Michael's land bordered the priest's land, and there was a path through one of Michael's fields which the priest's herdsman used to take as a short cut to the well. Michael stopped him one day and said he would prefer him to take the long way through the priest's own land. He went up to the priest's house and explained that he did not want to create a right of way through his land, in case he ever had to sell it. The priest did not see things that way. He regarded this request as an insult. Why should anyone stop him from going where he wanted to go?

'I suppose if it was me taking the short cut, you'd stop me as well?' the priest asked.

'I would,' Michael replied.

On the next Sunday, from the altar, the priest's sermon was about respect for the clergy and how this was one of the commandments of the Church.

'There are people in this parish,' the priest thundered, 'aye, even in this church, who do not treat their own priest, their own friend, with dignity.' Everybody knew to whom he was referring. 'Well, let me tell you this. They will have no luck in this world or the next. The grass will be growing at their door one day. Their house will be empty and there will be none of their spawn in it.'

It so happened that Michael Canavan never married. After his parents died, he lived on alone, quiet and embittered. People shook their heads and said, 'You should never cross the priest.'

Sometimes there were unexpected marriages. One day, when I came into the kitchen, my sisters were all in a flurry of excitement, especially my sister Rose. She was to be a bridesmaid. Imagine! A real bridesmaid at a wedding. Peggy Lacy was getting married in Claran Church on Friday. The Lacys were our cousins. Peggy's uncle was the one who had died when we heard the three knocks on the parlour door at three in the morning. Sudden death, sudden marriage: they were a sudden kind of family.

'On Friday, only three days away! What will you wear?'

'I have no clothes!'

'You will have to buy some.'

'Oh, you lucky thing. I wish I could be a bridesmaid.'

'You'll have to get shoes.'

'And a hat!'

'Oh my God!'

They went on like this for ages. I thought it was a big fuss over nothing. Rose was dispatched in haste to Headford and came home with boxes lined with tissue paper and brown-paper parcels. She got a new pink dress and white shoes and a hat that perched precariously on the side of her head and had to be attached with a big pin. She was on top of the world. She would be the real focus of attention, not the bride, who was quite plain.

Friday came, and with it harsh reality. The church was empty except for the bride and groom, the priest, and another man who was the groomsman. Neither of the two families concerned was present. Rose stood in dazed splendour in her pink dress and white shoes while the words of the ceremony echoed through the empty church. When it was all over, the bride and groom got into separate cars and went to their separate homes. We were at the head of the boreen, ready to light the customary wisp of celebration. When we saw the two cars leave the church, we were ready to strike the match, but they turned at the crossroads and went a different way. Then we saw Rose walking home in her pink dress, carrying the bouquet. She was not at all happy. Neither were we. As she passed by, we lit the fire anyway. She chased us angrily. She threw the bouquet in the fire and ran to the house.

After some time, the priest called the groom's parents to the presbytery and coaxed and cajoled them into agreeing to take in their new daughter-in-law. They were not too happy. The house was full already. But they gave in finally. Rose never got to show off the pink dress. It was not the colour for the town hall.

FINDING A SPACE

Though I grew up in the wide-open spaces of the west of Ireland, and though we had our secret places, in little fields with high hedges and lengthy shadows on the grass, there was never a place where you could be certain that you were alone. The land was accessible and the sky was wide and there was always the sound of human voices, calling the calves or turning the horse at the headland or rounding up the sheep. You never knew when someone would appear through the gap in the hedge and startle you with a greeting.

And then we got a bathroom. We had a dry toilet at the top of the haggard, made of galvanise, with a wooden seat and a bolt on the door, but you could not stay in there for long. In the summer you baked inside in two minutes flat, and the residue in the bucket greeted you well before you got to the door. In winter, it was freezing in that iron hut.

Most of the time we went up to the *páirc bheag* our business, with a good big dock leaf in hand. Then we had to be extra careful of being discovered. It was not a place you could send visitors from America. Finally, my father decided to build a bathroom on to the house.

There was a flurry of bathroom-building in rural Ireland in the late 'fifties. There were grants going, and my father was tired, too, of drawing water in barrels from the well. So the foundations were dug for the septic tank and the pipes across the haggard, and a discreet lean-to was added onto the back of the thatched house.

There were some teething problems, and the local plumber, who had been virtually unknown up to that time, suddenly attained the status of a witch doctor in the tribe. He was a crabbed little old man, with blue dungarees and a handlebar moustache. I think he felt that this new boom in bathroom-building had come too late in his career.

He cursed roundly as he tried to clear our sewerage pipes one sultry August afternoon. 'I don't mind them using paper,' he muttered, coming up for air, 'but they don't have to use the whole bloody *Connaught Tribune!*'

But we soon got used to our gleaming new space, with its tiled floor, full-length mirror and shiny white accoutrements. Bathrooms became the main subject of fireside talk. Old people, they said, were slow to adapt. A simple man from Carranriardra was reputed to have told a neighbour about the new device in the bathroom his son had built. It was for washing your feet, he said. You washed one foot, pulled a chain, 'and you had a clean sup for the next foot.'

As for me, a new era had opened up. In our house of ten children, bedrooms were a bit like railway stations. Somebody was always passing through.

Nobody could really stake territory. Before the arrival of the bathroom, there had been nowhere to storm off to and sulk, nowhere to read that well-thumbed book or the letter you had got from the girl in boarding school; and when the slanting rain swept in from the Corrib, drenching the hawthorns and the hedges, there was nowhere to have that illicit cigarette.

Now all was changed, changed utterly. We had a room with a lock. It was the only lock in the house, for no door was ever locked, not even at night. When you are a young teenager trying to decide which persona is right for you, it is vital that you have a space with a mirror and a lock. I could be James Dean or Frank Sinatra. I could practise the Elvis shuffle without seeming a complete idiot, and I remember sliding that new brass bolt home and thinking how ironic it was that a lock could be a key to a new life.

THE WRITTEN WORD REMAINS

'Nobody should keep a diary, or an autograph book either,' my mother said. 'The written word remains.'

I had just cycled the three miles home from secondary school, by the honeysuckle's smell in the hedges, to a dinner of fried potatoes and thick, home-cured rashers. Whatever about the odd parental lecture, at least I didn't have to face incarceration in a freezing boarding school. Three years earlier, the nuns had taken a courageous leap forward by admitting boys into the local convent day school. God only knows what heated exchanges had taken place in mother houses and wainscoted diocesan rooms. This was the west of Ireland, it was the mid-'fifties, and we were the first co-educational secondary school west of the Shannon.

The pioneering nuns took us in, country louts that we were, dusted the hayseed from our trousers, and gave us Latin and French and apologetics and pi-times-the-radius-squared. In no time at all we could match the girls in every subject. If only we could communicate with them.

The girl who owned the diary was from the town.

She sat in front of me in class and when she laughed, she threw back her head and the ends of her blonde hair just touched the top of my desk. She could never do a geometry cut, but she went to grown-up dances in the town hall, and she could jive better than anyone I knew. Her diary, which had a red padded cover with a gold clasp, also had a special pull-out section for autographs, and this was the one that was passed around the class. Now, maybe we were too shy to converse with the girls face to face, but given that vital few moments' reflection, we could communicate our thoughts in writing. Terrible, wild thoughts, things we could never dream of saying. Words borrowed from the street corner on a fair day, where we had learned terms and tales we scarcely understood. We signed our names under daring lines of lewdness. Then, of course, came the inevitable seizure by the vigilant nun, and the fearful court martial afterwards.

I remember waiting with sweaty palms for my turn to face the inquisition. Death seemed like a welcome alternative to the possibility of disclosure. Luckily, my contribution was quite low on the Richter scale of shockingness. The letter home was mild enough.

Looking back now, there was really very little to cause a raised eyebrow, but the guardians of innocence were vigilant in those days and the least crack in the sea wall was sealed quickly to ward off any threat that might exist from an unknown tide.

Thirty years have slipped by since then, and I'm rummaging through that old shoebox in the top of my wardrobe – the thing I would look for if I knew the house was on fire. There is a diary here that I'm glad I have. Words written by a child of mine who must have found it easier to write them than to say them. Though she's no longer here, her words, defeating time and space, will stay with me forever.

That's why I'm all for diaries. Let the written word remain.

PHOTOGRAPHS

Time doth transfix the flourish set on youth,
And delves the parallels on Beauty's brow;
Feeds on the rarities of Nature's truth,
And nothing stands but for its scythe to mow.

Shakespeare's old sonnet brings me back through days
and distance to the schoolroom with the high windows
in Headford long ago, where we struggled with Latin
verbs and the vagaries of the ablative absolute.

Our Latin teacher never succeeded in teaching me
much Latin, but I was very lucky to have him and he
taught us about life and waking into a world that was
changing at a dizzying pace in those last dying days
of the 'fifties. And he taught us about time.

Like most teachers of his era he was strict and
diligent; we learned or suffered the consequences, but
he was more interested in ideas than in facts and he
was easily diverted from the narrow confines of the
curriculum that sought to bind him. He loved to discuss
films and plays he had seen and he revelled in the
moral dilemmas that faced Fletcher Christian and

Brutus and Hamlet, Prince of Denmark. He wanted to share his experience with us, and we tried our best to encourage him as often as possible. Anything was better than Latin grammar.

Which brings me to that memorable morning when he was at his best. We were struggling with Roman history, and the Great Punic War and Hannibal's army marching on Rome, and a wily Roman general called Fabius Cunctator, which means, as I recall, 'The One Who Delays'.

Fabius just lurked in the hills and only sniped at the tail end of Hannibal's army. He then disappeared into the hills again and waited for another opportunity to attack, infuriating the poor Carthaginians and finally wearing them down – and saving Rome in the process. I suppose he was one of the first exponents of guerrilla warfare. Time was on his side, you see.

And of course, we got talking about time and what it meant to different people, and then the teacher asked the basic question 'What is time?' so we really had to think. He loved to see us wrestle with the concept in our own simple way.

'Think of a photograph of the class,' he said, 'and another photograph you might take after a few minutes. What would be the difference? Somebody would have moved, wouldn't they?'

And in his own thoughtful, skilful way he led us to the conclusion that time is really a measurement of movement of change. We calculate the motion of the Earth and divide it into units with names like 'days' and 'years'. But if there was no movement, there would be no such thing as time. By way of illustration, he produced a newspaper from his desk and showed us a great action picture from the sports page of a horse in full flight over Becher's Brook.

'A photograph freezes all movement,' he said. 'A photograph conquers time.'

Those of us who have lost somebody precious know how right he was. When, suddenly, many years later, death snatched our daughter Caroline from us, one of our first mesmerised reactions was to scour the house for photographs: evidence that she had been among us. There were never enough of them: shots of camping trips and dressing up for Hallowe'en and opening presents on Christmas morning, each picture more precious than a jewel. Time frozen in a moment; moments locked in the memory.

A LIZARD DANCING

Jim Maguire and I went to all the dances together, except for that night in Seapoint, the night it happened. I was in the back of a Hillman Minx and we were parked right at the spot. Joe Hynes had given me a lift to the dance and when I met the blonde with the beehive hairdo he gave me the keys. Her lacquered hair was stuck to my jaw and I was lost in the warmth of her angora jumper when I heard the commotion. I wiped the condensation from the rear window to see what was going on.

Jim Maguire stood in the middle of the street with his hand held up like a policeman on point duty. Cars leaving the dance had to brake suddenly, or swerve to avoid him. Passengers jeered loudly at him from the open windows and some of the men tried to land a punch on him as they passed by, but he was able to dance nimbly out of their way. Sometimes he would sweep his left hand round like a matador as a car drove by, only to jump straight into the path of the next car, forcing it to a screeching halt.

When he bounded towards a group of girls on the

pavement, they scattered in all directions, but he caught the girl in the red coat just like you would corner a sheep for shearing. He tried to kiss her.

'Get off me, you big lunatic. Let me go!' she screamed.

He turned her around and tried to look into her face as she twisted away from him, kicking at his shins. Her friends came back with two men and they pushed him away. He stepped back onto the road and shadow-boxed, weaving and bobbing.

'Come on then, come on!' he bellowed like a bull. The passing headlights picked out his widening eyes, the spittle on his mouth and the sweat glistening on his broad forehead. Then, suddenly, between moments of light, he disappeared into the night. It was such a shock to see him like that, changed into another person, like an actor totally transformed on stage.

I should have seen it coming. Earlier that night, when I was upstairs in the balcony with the beehive blonde, watching the swaying mass of humanity on the dance floor below us, I picked him out, on the edge of the dancers. He was moving along the line of girls who stood at the pillars. I watched them all shake their heads or just avert their faces when he asked them to dance.

Later, as I waited outside the ladies' cloakroom, I stood behind a pillar and avoided him. 'Save the Last Dance for Me' blared out from inside the swing doors. He was just standing there on the steps of the porch, watching the men who waited smugly for their women. The blast of heat and the smell of sweat and perfume from within met the cold wind that blew in from outside, bringing the pungent odour of the sea and the smell of chips and vinegar from the stalls along the promenade. The women came out newly made up, nervous, eyes straight ahead. The men kept their eyes on the cloakroom door, trying to remember a face. They would pair off and head out for the eternal ritual in the parked car or the darkened shelter by the seafront.

Jim just stared with a dazed, forlorn expression on his face. This was a game for which he had not been picked. I felt uneasy, but then the girl with the beehive hairdo came out, all made up and smiling. I turned up the collar of my coat and went out with her, keeping my back to him, as if I did not know he was there.

'My God, what the hell happened to you?' Joe Hynes asked, opening the door of the car. Marty Connolly was with him, looking for a lift home. 'Did you pluck her or what?'

My coat was all white hairs from her angora jumper, but I wore them proudly, as a badge of conquest.

'Did you see Jim Maguire?' Joe asked.

'He went cracked altogether!'

I muttered that I had seen it all.

'He was always cracked if you ask me,' Marty said, settling himself into the front seat.

'How could he be any other way?' Joe added, starting up the car and fixing the tails of his coat under him in the seat.

'Sure 'tisn't from the wind he brought it.'

'He won't get into the guards now, even if he does make the height,' Marty cackled smugly.

Everybody in the town knew the story. Nancy Maguire was determined to get her son into the guards, but he was just a fraction short of the five foot nine inches required. At least that was Sergeant Malone's excuse. Nancy heard 'The Answer Man' on radio say that people were taller when they were asleep, so one morning at half past seven she ran down to the station shouting, 'Measure him now while he's hot!'

I tried to change the conversation and wiped away some more of the condensation from the window. The stone walls and bushes and trees flickered through the stark image of my own face in the glass looking back at me, and then it became his face, all wounded and frightened and vulnerable, like a rabbit caught in a snare. As we left the bright lights of the city behind and headed for home, I wondered where he was and how he would get back. I felt a sharp pain in my stomach, as if there was a lizard gnawing at my gut. It was my last summer at home, and the two of us had been inseparable.

'Who are you going to the dance with?' my father would enquire whenever I asked him for the pound note on a Sunday evening.

'Jim Maguire,' I would answer, and then I would see a look on his face as if he wanted to take back the money.

'Have you nobody else to go with?'

The Maguires' place was bordering ours on the Ballyhale side. We worked 'in co' with horses and mowing machines and labour on the farm. But Jim was not much of a farmer. One day when we were castrating calves Jim just wandered off, letting the calves go careering out of the pen. His father said that was typical of him. Some days he would be gone for hours with that black-and-white collie dog of his while his father ranted and raved and called him all the names under the sun. There was a small deep turlough sheltered by hawthorn bushes between our two farms that my father used to call 'The Swallow Hole'. He said that if something fell in there it would never be found. I often saw Jim there standing at the brink looking in. Not skidding stones like we did as kids, but just staring into the dark brown water.

But there was something about him that struck a chord in me, and when we were together we could laugh at the world, as if it was all a circus and we were in the back-row seats. We could talk about things the others never heard of. He had never made it to secondary school but he read *Wide World* magazine and *Reader's Digest* and he remembered everything he read. Joe Hynes, who read nothing except maybe *Old Moore's Almanac,* was always ready to poke fun at him. So was everybody else, I suppose. Jim's younger brother was a genius at school and got the county council scholarship, but that only made them nod wisely and mutter about the hair's breadth.

When Joe dropped me off in the village that night, I walked past the darkened houses and the curtained windows. I had a strong urge to break them all, so that people would rush out onto the street and I could jeer them for looking so stupid. When I got to my own room it felt like a prison. For the first time, I was glad that I would soon be leaving home. I felt grown up, and I knew that it should have felt good, but it did not. When I finally closed my eyes, sleep stole up like a slow dark cloud spreading from the back of my head but the scene on the street outside the dance hall flickered away like an old Chaplin movie. Jim Maguire was the clown and the boxer and the madman too and I was shooting the scene from the back of the Hillman Minx, through the gap in the condensation. In every close-up, his wide eyes looked at me with fear and accusation.

I went out with Vera, the beehive blonde, for what remained of that last summer in the west. I met Jim only occasionally at dance halls and marquees, and I did my best to pretend that nothing had changed but there was a veil across his eyes and a strange twist to his smile. He would not try to dance; he would just stand there, at the every edge of the dance floor, staring at the couples who swayed and glided effortlessly by him. He looked like a would-be passenger on the platform of a foreign railway station with no ticket home.

In late September I finally got the call to the civil service and headed off for Dublin, and another life. I met him once or twice during my holidays and there was the inevitable awkward effort at reminiscence and the promise to meet for a drink, but by now he was firmly locked away in his own prison and his eyes were fixed on that blank wall before him. I was already on the outside, a refracted soul. There was no way back for either of us. If anybody ever joined in our stumbling efforts at conversation, there was the knowing nod and smile at whatever he said, as if he were a failed professor who had once tried to prove a crazy theory.

I'm on the phone to my mother on a grey day in November, looking out the window of the office at the top of Westmoreland Street, and the traffic is building up as rush hour approaches. She's telling me all the local news and it is unreal to me now, and I'm not really interested, though I pretend to be.

'And Jim Maguire, you remember him, don't you? He left home. He just wandered off and disappeared. Nobody knows where he is. They think he might be gone to England, although some say that he might have done away with himself, the Lord save us! We don't know what to think. Are you still there?'

The traffic out there is cruel and I'm thinking that they would need a guard on point duty, and for a split second I think I see him there in the middle of the street, the wintry sun picking out his blond head, bobbing and weaving, and his hand in the air trying to attract the attention of the people whizzing by in their insulated cars, each one locked in their own isolation, warm but incapable of warmth. Then the sun disappears behind a big leaden cloud and my own startled image catches me again from the glass, and the glass becomes the surface of the turlough in Ballyhale.

And down in that brown pool I can see the yellow lizard that is dancing in my gut.

Winds of Change

The day came when a line of long, straight black poles marched down the hill into the green valley like an invading army, carrying curving wires and bringing irreversible change to an old world. The gentle rounded corners of shadow in the kitchen were sharpened by the glare of artificial light. The row of jugs on the dresser did not glint individually in the light of a candle any more but stared back as one. The darkness outside became blacker once you had left the brightness of the kitchen. The cow's eyes bulged with brightness bordering on fear when the light in the cow-byre was switched on. Old people said that the milk would never be the same.

My brother Pat talked to the men who came to dig the holes for the myriad of electricity poles. They spoke of the money that was to be earned: good wages for simple work. He saw and he heard and he thought of the plough and the harrow and the scuffler and the grinding hardship of earning a living on a small farm. No money in your pocket except on a fair day, when you might sell a bullock. He told my father he wanted to go with these new labourers for a while. My father narrowed his eyes and looked along the line of poles to where they disappeared over Carrowbeg hill, and he must have known then that this new invading army would steal his son away for good.

My brother Michael took over the work of the farm, but my father's patience at teaching the skills of the plough was wearing thin. He became fractious and bad-tempered. He had taught my sister, Cecile, to farm as well as the best, and she had left when she was ready. Now Pat, who was seen as the heir to the old farm, who had acquired all the skills and who had seemed so interested in it, had been lured away by the new world. My father was getting old and tired.

Eventually, Michael got tired, too, of all the complaining about drills not being straight and old farming methods that were fast becoming a thing of the past. The tractor had taken over, the combine harvester now tied the sheaves, and the weeds were sprayed, not dug up. Michael headed for Galway, where industry was beginning to boom, and became a plumber. His twin brother, Jim, left school and for a while worked the farm happily with the old man, both of them content and compatible. But it was a short, unreal interlude. They both knew it would not last. Jim left to become a policeman. I was gone to college. My father retreated into the house, into himself. He sat by the window and saw the weeds grow in the fields where he had proudly worked. He saw the straight, stately walls breach and fall in places. He struggled to rebuild them, but the stones became too heavy for him.

He was getting the old-age pension, and so was my mother, and they lived the last years of their lives with my sister Julia in the house where they had reared us all. The house we had filled with the noise of laughter and argument and tears and anger and all the sounds of growing up was now virtually silent except for the dripping of rain from the thatch and the flapping of the ivy by the window. The plough became rusty by the glass wall. The stone stands in the haggard stood tenantless. The cow-byre and the horses' stable were empty. My mother did not keep hens any more; she bought them from the traveling shop. She also had a fridge by then, so she could buy frozen peas and milk. My brother Michael, adept at the plumbing now, installed an iron range in the kitchen, blocking off the open fire, with its wide archway and hobs where I had first sat and heard my Aunt Molly tell me the story of the Butt of the Wind. Now they would have constant hot water and the house would not be full of draughts.

And so my father and mother were left alone with the special child they loved especially. Their thoughts strayed often, I am sure, to their meetings in the dawn by the chapel field in Carnacrow, when they were young in the old world, and I am certain that no iron stove, no running water, no sharpness of light, no invading army of poles ever erased the memories of the love they planted in that house in the green valley.

LOST FOR WORDS

My father is dying. I have come down from Dublin for the weekend to take my turn at his bedside. Three of my older sisters are here, but they are exhausted, having stayed up for nights on end. My brothers have come and gone, so it is time for the youngest of the family to do his stint. My mother wanders about the house aimlessly, fussing over anything that might keep her mind off the prospect of his death. He is eighty-six years old and she is already lost without him.

My father is in the narrow bedroom just off the kitchen. It has a small, cast-iron fireplace and a wall-cupboard where he used to keep his cut-throat razor and his shaving brush in a shiny silver box. The strop hung on the back of the door. I remember the sharpening and the scented smell, the bright steel dipping into the steaming water in the white enamel basin on the washstand, the way he pulled the skin taught with his left hand to make the bristles stand up, the gleaming blade cleaning the sunburnt neck. On the opposite side of the room there is an old polished chiffonier with a bevel-edged mirror. It was my mother's dowry when she came from Carnacrow. Out of the big house to this low, thatched cottage to be with this big man who now looks so skeletal and white.

He is drifting in and out of consciousness, making low moans deep down in his throat as if he were talking to an unknown spirit. He makes no sign of recognition, but just keeps trying to turn his face to the wall. His eyes tighten into a painful frown as he tries to pull the catheter our from under the bedclothes. I have to stop him. He pushes against me, but he has barely any strength left. I think of how he used to shoulder two-hundredweight bags of corn up the stone stairway to the barn, how he used to land the big steel plough into the back of the horse-cart in one great, grunting heave.

I take a Q-tip from the table beside the bed, dip it in the glass of water and hold it to his lips. He sucks the moisture greedily, like a baby. I think of him downing the first long draught of porter when I would take him to Ryder's on a Sunday night.

'Arragh, wouldn't you get up at night to drink it!' he would say, licking his lips. And on nights like that I would not feel the distance between us, would not feel crowded out by others. But he always knew when to draw down the shutter.

'Drink up that and we'll be going home,' he would say, reaching uneasily for this cap, as if there was something in the next drink that he feared.

Now, on his deathbed, I offer him another drink from the tiny cotton swab as his lips part, but he turns his head sideways, makes a face and groans as a long, dry rattle sounds in his throat. He craves the moisture but he cannot swallow. Death is playing its final cruel hand. He leans his head back on the bed and I bend over him, trying to fix the pillows.

Suddenly his whole body stiffens and he fixes me with a wide-eyed stare, as if he had just woke up suddenly from a strange and terrifying dream. There is a rattle in his throat and I know that he is trying to speak. I lean my ear low to his lips.

'There's an old football in the shed,' he says haltingly through rasping breaths. 'You'll have to pump it up.'

But the sudden revival lasts only a few seconds before he closes his eyes with a kind of resigned, languorous dropping of the eyelids and turns away from me once more to face the wall. I stand up, dumbfounded, and look out through the lace curtains at the small field in front of the house where we used to play football. In the gloaming of a summer Sunday evening, Dinnie Molloy and John Biggins and the Greaneys from Culleen would gather. I can see the road gate where he stood that evening with Canon Curley, watching us.

'Your lad is very fast, Mick,' I could hear the priest say after I had jinked my way past flailing arms to score a goal.

'He would need to toughen up a bit,' I could hear my father say. 'He's too small.'

I remember, years later, coming off the field in Tuam Stadium after winning the county final. If only he had come and shaken my hand. I turn again to the huddled, broken form on the bed. I lean over him and listen, but there is only that dry rattle in the throat.

My mother comes into the room. 'Any improvement?' she asks anxiously.

I shake my head and move past her in the narrow doorway, through the dark kitchen and out into the hazy June sunshine to wander in familiar places.

His ghost is everywhere, even while he is still alive. I can see him stumbling through the haggard with a rope of hay on his back, or crouched at the top of the ladder thatching the neatly coned stack of wheat as if it was a house that would have to withstand a deluge, pointing the scollops and pushing them in with a grunt of satisfaction as if he was a surgeon stitching up a wound. When I look up towards the High Graffa I see his stooped form behind the plough, his head cocked to one side to judge the straightness of the furrow, the peaked cap pushed back on his head.

My father died at half past three the next morning, without speaking another word to anyone.

The following day the neighbours gathered, the men drink whiskey in the scullery and said what a tough man he was and how well he reared his family through the hard days of compulsory tillage and the Economic War and food rationing. When I got a moment alone with him in the room, I kissed his cold, hollow cheek that I had earlier tried to shave with my safety razor. I found it strange, kissing him. I took his cold, stiff hand and clasped it in a firm handshake. Then I held him by the wasted shoulders in our only remembered embrace.

Three days later I am in the barn, moping around. I should have returned to Dublin by now but I am putting it off as long as I can. The barn has an air of musty decay about it, in sharp contrast to the way it used to be when the wool was being packed, or the pig salted, or the oats being winnowed in the breeze between the two doors. Now there is an old electric cooker, its door hanging open, standing in the middle of the floor. The old workbench that he made is in the corner, its vice open and rusted like some fossilised monster. Beside the bench there is a big brown wardrobe, thrown out because of the dry rot, a broken shovel propped against the door to keep it closed. I lift the shovel and the door swings open and something rolls out onto the floor: a football, worn to a thread and almost flat. It is one of the old-style ones, with a teat that had to be doubled back and tied before stuffing it back inside the cover, which then had to be laced.

In a kind of daze of remembrance, I wander in to the house and take down the blue jug from the dresser. I find, under some unpaid bills, a tool that looks like a screwdriver; only the blade is not a blade, but a kind of inverted packing needle. It is the stitcher he made for us, for lacing up the ball. I root around in the bottom of the jug. There used to be a bicycle valve that he had specially cut from an old tube so that it would fit into the teat of the ball in such a way that the ball could be inflated.

The phone rings and it is my wife, calling from Dublin. She wants to know if I'll be home by Saturday. My son is to play a soccer match. 'I wonder should I

247

get him the new boots?' she asks. 'There's a pair at twenty-five quid that I think are fine, but nothing will do him but the dearer ones.'

I cannot get involved in the conversation. It all seems so far away. Here in the old parlour, my voice sounds hollow and I feel as if I'm speaking from inside a deep, dry well.

'Will I get them, do you think?'

She puts young Mark on. 'I'll be wearing number seven, Da, like Roy Keane.'

I wanted to say, 'That's fantastic, son', but the words just would not come out.

The Knell of Parting Day

I went to visit my mother in the nursing home in Corrandula. It was a converted monastery, a place near home, but not like home, a place of quiet sadness. She sat alone in a shaft of slanting sunlight, forgetting where she was, or who I was, but when the bell rang down the corridor and through the silence between us, she piped up in her frail, lilting voice: 'The curfew tolls the knell of parting day.' Even in the desert of her failing faculties, there is an oasis of poetry within her that remains forever green.

I think of her schooldays in that old two-roomed schoolhouse overlooking Lough Corrib, of the school book I searched for in the vaults of the Educational Company of Ireland. I knew she would have used such a book. When at last I found it I felt that it was somehow sacred and when I opened its worn brown covers I was transported back across the changing years to a time before independence, a time of poverty of the body and richness of the soul. From between its fragile pages her childhood unfolded like the petals of a pressed flower coming to life again and all the magisterial poems and noble prose in that old book were, I felt, a kind of testament to the nobility and pride of her now vanishing generation.

There was an old order there, a lesson in every story, a moral in every verse. There was love of country, but no lust for blood or battle, only a burning pride in one's own birthplace. These were the days before we got our own bloodied hands on the plough of nationhood, before Béal na Bláth, before Angel Dust and holes in the ozone layer, before we built nursing homes for our mothers who had reared their families: our salad days when we were 'green in judgement'.

As we sit together now in that quiet, echoing place, I see that her mind is failing her fast. She rummages through her locker and takes out a little notebook.

'Jim was here on Monday.'

She writes everything down now, because she knows her memory is gone. She takes up the pen to record my visit. I watch the sinews spreading from wrist to knuckle of her gnarled hand like the filaments of a web. I see the image of the lifelines spreading outwards from her heart that always held us, each one of her family, since the moment of our first cry. This web, this net that she spun, was always there to save us. It was soft as silk and yet tempered as tungsten, forged in prayer that she whispered alone in the dim light of her room under the dripping thatch of Ivy Cottage. What will happen to us when she steals away from the centre? We will be lost.

She has been a lost soul since the man of her heart has passed away. We visited her with our children and she fussed over them as usual, but there was a space about her that nobody could fill, a distance in her sad eyes that gazed beyond us to a place we could never see. She took to getting up at night and wandering about the house, bumping into thinks in the dark. One morning, early, she fell against the old chiffonier in her bedroom. Her head was badly cut. We knew then that she could not live in the old house any more. Julia would not be able to look after her by herself.

So she moved to this quiet place among strangers. She did not like it, but she resigned herself to the inevitable, as she always had in her life. She took up her beads and prayed for us all, shared our troubles and prepared herself for her last days.

Those days came quickly enough. As she lay on her deathbed she held my hand in hers and said: 'The clock stopped, never to go again.'

I think of the clock in the parlour of Ivy Cottage, the one flanked by the bronze figures of the sower and the reaper. I gaze into her eyes and thank her silently for what she has sown. She slips quietly away.

The Lonely Traveller's Call

My brother still phones home every Christmas, even
though he knows there is nobody at the other end of
the line. Our parents have passed on, but the family
house has remained untouched, poised uneasily
between generations. My brother is ringing from
Wichita, Kansas, four and a half thousand miles away
in the great open prairies of America. He has lived and
worked there since he boarded the transatlantic liner
in Cobh as a fresh-faced seminarian missionary in 1951.

He left the old thatched homestead where the
shadows of the oil lamp softened the kitchen, and
returned, four years later, on his first visit, to the age
of the electric light. And with each successive trip
home, he noticed another piece missing from the
remembered picture of his childhood.

But he never managed to come home from the States
for Christmas, so for him that early mystical time
remains intact, unspoilt by time or change. When he
thinks of Christmas night, he still thinks of the big
supper, with the red candle in the window, the green
sprig of holly behind each picture in the whitewashed

kitchen, and my father's annual tongue-in-cheek prayer from the top of the table: 'This time next year, if there are no more of us, may there be no less of us.'

For my brother, Christmas will forever be as it was then – a time when he knew the shelter and the warmth of human love, felt certain about it, took it for granted, like the fire on the hearth.

Now, though the fire is quenched and the hearth is cold and the only family he was ever a part of is scattered, my brother still makes that phone-call home each Christmas night. He just lets that old black phone ring out at the other end of the line and imagines the sound echoing through the dark, empty parlour where the lace curtains hang white and ghostlike in the gloom.

I'm sure he finds it difficult to explain his strange yearly compulsion, but I think I understand. I know, for one thing, that imagination is more powerful than fact, and that memory needs its own rituals, especially at this time, when the ghost of Christmas past peers through the cracks in that great veneer of festivity that surrounds us.

I believe my brother knows that Christmas is a time for missing those we have lost and giving solace to the lonely soul within us. And when he hears the phone ring, I'm sure there are voices that answer, and faces that take shape again out of the shadow of the lamp, and Christmas smells that waft in from the old parlour and make him live again, for a fleeting fragment of time, through the provident simplicity that was our Christmas childhood.

And in that vision of an unchanged and still

unchanging past, when, across oceans and time and space, he connects again with the souls of all that he has loved, what need is there for words?